Routledge Revivals

Palestine of the Jews

Palestine of the Jews (1919) examines the history of Jewish Palestine, from 4,000 years ago to the early twentieth century and the Balfour Declaration. It details the importance of Palestine to the Jews, it being for two thousand years the centre of their nation, and for two thousand more the centre of their hopes and aspirations.

Palestine of the Jews

Past, Present, and Future

Norman Bentwich

First published in 1919
by Kegan Paul, Trench, Trubner & Co. Ltd.

This edition first published in 2025 by Routledge
4 Park Square, Milton Park, Abingdon, Oxon, OX14 4RN

and by Routledge
605 Third Avenue, New York, NY 10017

Routledge is an imprint of the Taylor & Francis Group, an informa business

All rights reserved. No part of this book may be reprinted or reproduced or utilised in any form or by any electronic, mechanical, or other means, now known or hereafter invented, including photocopying and recording, or in any information storage or retrieval system, without permission in writing from the publishers.

Publisher's Note
The publisher has gone to great lengths to ensure the quality of this reprint but points out that some imperfections in the original copies may be apparent.

Disclaimer
The publisher has made every effort to trace copyright holders and welcomes correspondence from those they have been unable to contact.

A Library of Congress record exists under LCCN 19003155

ISBN: 978-1-032-90387-3 (hbk)
ISBN: 978-1-003-55775-3 (ebk)
ISBN: 978-1-032-90392-7 (pbk)

Book DOI 10.4324/9781003557753

PALESTINE OF THE JEWS

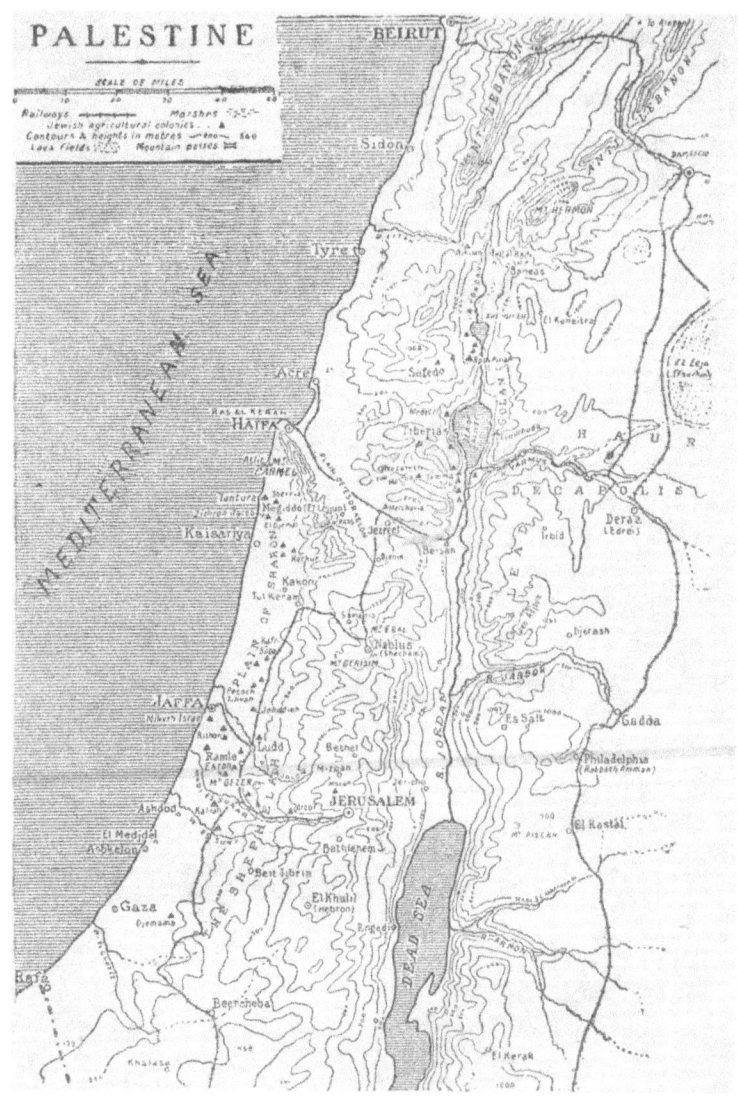

PALESTINE [*Front*

PALESTINE OF THE JEWS

PAST, PRESENT, AND FUTURE

BY

NORMAN BENTWICH
EGYPTIAN EXPEDITIONARY FORCE

Author of "Josephus" and
"Philo-Judæus of Alexandria"

WITH AN APPENDIX
THE REDEMPTION OF JUDÆA
AND OTHER ARTICLES ON THE BRITISH ADVANCE

LONDON
KEGAN PAUL, TRENCH, TRUBNER & Co. Ltd.
BROADWAY HOUSE, 68–74 CARTER LANE, E.C.
1919

PREFACE

This little book has been written during the leisure hours of camp life in the Summer of 1917 while waiting at the portals of Palestine to enter the Promised Land. It is based on notes which I had jotted down in the country during several visits in the years before the war. As, between 1916 and 1917, we slowly crossed the Wilderness of Sinai in which the Hebrew tribes had wandered nearly 4000 years ago, I would often meditate at night under the starry sky upon the past and the future of my people who have wandered now over the world for nigh two thousand years. When vision was limited, reflection and reminiscence helped the lingering hours to pass, and when action was checked I would dream of what might be when Israel was restored to his home. Like the camels I was leading over the desert, I would chew the cud of memory when the day's work was done, and the gentle evening breathed peace and tranquillity.

My stray notes which I have put together in these circumstances may perchance help to make better known the rebirth of the Jewish people, and the regeneration of the historic land of Israel, which has been happening in the last half-century. As a great French writer has said, "La verité a toujours quelque chose de l'inattendu qui la rend supportable," and my reason for adding to the inexhaustible literature of Palestine is that I have tried to tell the simple tale of what has been achieved by a small remnant of the oldest nationality.

For more than two years I have been far from books and papers, which do not find a place in a marching kit, even with the generous allowance of 50 lbs. of baggage; and I must crave indulgence on that account for any inaccuracies and mistakes. I have made no attempt to be exhaustive in the account of the Jewish settlement, and I have given only my personal experience. To my father I owe it that my pencilled notes have been prepared for publication, with the assistance of my sister and her husband, who were among the colonisers before the war. And I am indebted to the same ready help for the incorporation in the text of references to the more salient later developments, so as to bring the work more nearly up to date.

PALESTINE, $\frac{1918}{5678}$ NORMAN BENTWICH.

POSTSCRIPT.—The Appendix, containing a series of Sketches on the British Advance to Jerusalem, is added by kind permission of the Proprietors of the *Manchester Guardian*, to which they were originally contributed, a short Article on "The Redemption of Judæa" published in *Palestine* (the organ of the British Palestine Committee) being also included. And the Map which forms the Frontispiece is, by courtesy of the proprietors, taken from the larger map specially prepared for the latter publication.

CONTENTS

CHAPTER I

PALESTINE IN JEWISH HISTORY

The Place of Palestine in General History—The Exile and the Return—The Alexandrians and the Temple—The Maccabæan Struggle—Conquest by the Romans and Dispersion—Preservation of the Schools—Spread of Persecution—Persian Invasion and Capture of Jerusalem—Rise of Islam—The Crusades and the Latin Kingdom—Victory of Saladin—Maimonides, Al-Charisi, Nachmanides—Immigration of Spanish Refugees—New Settlements in Galilee—False Messiahs—Sabbatai Zevi and the Donmeh—The Millenarian Movement in England—Return of Scholars to the Holy Cities . 1–20

CHAPTER II

THE MODERN ZIONIST MOVEMENT

The French Revolution—Civil Emancipation of the Jew—The Paris Sanhedrin and a Concordat—Napoleon's Manifesto to the Jews—Moses Mendelssohn—The Denationalisation Movement—Rise of Mehemet Ali—Sir Moses Montefiore and a Jewish Commonwealth—" Blood Accusation " at Damascus—Hess's " Rome and Jerusalem "—George Eliot and Dean Stanley on the Return—Disraeli and Lassalle—The Russian Persecutions—The

CONTENTS

"Lovers of Zion" Societies—Laurence Oliphant and a Gilead Scheme—Growth of the Palestine Communities—Rise of the National Movement—Herzl and the Basle Congress—Zionism and its "Financial Instrument"—El-Arish and Uganda—Opponents of Zionism—Spinoza on Jewish Development—A "Jewish Mission"—The Twentieth-Century View—Spread of the 'Palestine Sentiment—Declaration of the British Government of November 2nd, 1917—Position of the Jews at the Peace Congress . . . 21–48

CHAPTER III

THE AGRICULTURAL COLONIES: I. JUDÆA

Return of Jews to the Land—Their attachment to the Agricultural Life—Jewish Farmers in Russia and America—The Jewish Colonisation Association (I.C.A.)—Foundation of Agricultural Schools by the Alliance Israélite—The First Colony—"The Gate of Hope"—The Pioneers of Colonisation—The B.I.L.U.—Baron Edmond de Rothschild—Spread of the Colonies—Petach Tikvah—Working Men's Settlements—The Arab Labourers and the Yemenites—Religious and Social Life in the Colonies—The Sabbath Day—The Cultivation of Grapes and Oranges—The Great Wine Vaults—The "Carmel"—Spread of the Co-operative Principle—Rischon-le-Zion—Rechoboth: a progressive settlement—Government of the Village Communities—The Va-ad and Universal Suffrage—The Local Police (Shomerim)—Sanitation and Water Supply—Control of Education—The Government Tax—Local Taxation of Land Values—Schemes of Colonial Federation—Smaller Colonies (Katra)—Scholar-farmers and their outlook—A personal reminiscence—The New Judæa 49–77

CONTENTS

CHAPTER IV

THE COLONIES: II. SAMARIA AND THE NORTH

Local Patriotism in the Colonies—The Samarian group—Historical Associations—The Carmel Ridge—Zichron Jacob—Arab Cultivation, and the Jewish—Chederah—Athlit and Ancient Cæsarea—The Glass Factory of Tantura—Converts in the Colonies—The Jewish Agricultural Station—Scientific cultivation of the land—The Galilean Colonies—The Cornfields of the North—The Olive and Almond tree plantations — Jewish Labour Settlements—Merchavya—The Sabbatical Year and the Jubilee—Student-Colonists—Training Colonies—Medjdel, a Working-men's Colony—The Lake of Tiberias—Melchamyeh and Kinnereth—An American Plantation—" Achuzah " schemes—The " Corner Stone " (Rosh Pinah)—Metullah, a Summer Resort—An empty area—Fields for Enterprise — The Trans-Jordania Region — A Jewish Country—Work for the New Era   78–99

CHAPTER V

JERUSALEM

The religious character of the city—Its ancient history—Situation and outlook—The two Jerusalems—Growth of the suburbs—The Jewish population—The Bokharans' Community—The Yemenites and the Falashas—The Jewish Quarter—The Synagogues—The Karaites—The Wailing Wall—The Temple area—The Dome of the Rock—The Mount of Olives—The new Acropolis of the Jews—" Abraham's Vineyard "—The Montefiore Trust—The American Colony—Jewish historical sites—The Tomb of the Kings and of Rachel—The Pools of Solomon—Christian Jerusalem—Russian, German and French Monuments—The Church of the Holy Sepulchre—Custody of the Holy Places—Jew and Arab—Influence of the Holy City—A Temple of Peace—The Spiritual Metropolis of Mankind   100–128

CHAPTER VI

THE "HOLY CITIES" AND SEA OF GALILEE

Beauty of the Scenery—The Sea of the Harp (Kinnereth)—The Reconciliation of Nature—Galilee of the Gentiles—Ruins of great Cities—The Seat of the Post-Exilic Colleges—Crusaders' strongholds—The Horns of Hattin—Return of the Exiles—Safed, the "City set on a Hill"—The School of the Kabbala—Don Joseph of Naxos—Modern descendants of the old settlers—Kitchener's Survey—Tiberias and its Walls—The Market Place—The hot Springs of Tiberias—Along the banks of the Lake—First View of Safed—A Progressive Kaimakam—The Streets of Safed—Life in the Town—The Chaluka—Schools of the Alliance Israélite—Meiron, the Jewish pilgrimage place—The Zohar—The "Scholars' Feast"—Ruins of Ancient Synagogues—View from the heights—Mount Hermon—Banias, the source of the Jordan—Tyre and Sidon—The Lebanon Province—Growth of Beirut—A Jewish Province—The Pride of Israel   129–151

CHAPTER VII

THE RENAISSANCE IN THE SCHOOLS

The ideal Republic—The place of the Schools in Judaism—The Schools of the Ghetto—Growth of a new spirit—The modern Schools—Revival of the National tongue—Jewish culture in Palestine—The Talmud Torahs—Schools of the Alliance and the Hilfsverein—The Evelina de Rothschild School in Jerusalem—Kindergartens and Secondary Schools—The struggle for Hebrew—The Haifa Polytechnic—Fight for the Schools—The Jaffa Gymnasium—Religious Teaching in the Schools—Schools for Music and the Arts—The "Bezalel" School of Arts and Crafts—The War and the Schools—Palestinian Exiles at Alexandria—A National

CONTENTS

University in Jerusalem—El Azhar—The Spiritual hegemony of Palestine—The Zionist ideal—The return to Jewry—Setting up of the new Kingdom
152–177

CHAPTER VIII

THE WAR AND THE SETTLEMENTS

The Tripolitan and Balkan Wars—Ottoman Military Service—Projects of Reform—Commercial and Railway schemes—An American Commission—Outbreak of war in 1914—A financial crisis—Organisation of mutual help in the Jewish Colonies—Declaration of war against the Entente—A war of Peoples—Exodus of Jewish Settlers—America to the rescue—Egypt, the land of refuge—Suppression of Zionist institutions—Requisitions for the Turkish Army—A Plague of Locusts—Preservation of the Schools—Advance of the Brttish Army—Deportation of Jewish populations—Gaza and Jaffa—Distress in the Colonies—Famine prices in the Towns—The situation in Jerusalem—Fate of " the advance guard " of Jewry—A martyred land—Compensations of the War—Opening of the Land—Hopes of the People—The beginning of fulfilment 178–192

CHAPTER IX

THE FUTURE OF THE LAND AND THE PEOPLE

The Settlement of the Nations—Claims of the oldest nationality—Adoption of Zionism by the democracies of the world—Proposals for future Government of Palestine—A National Home for the Jews—The Spiritual Promise of Palestine—The meeting place of Continents—A network of Railways—Linking up the Near East and the Far East—Agricultural and mineral wealth of the country—

xvi   CONTENTS

      Schemes of irrigation—Electric power for industrial development—Harnessing the rivers—The Jordan Valley — The Historical Boundaries — Conder's estimate of Palestine's possibilities—The Land of the Promise—Gilead and Moab—A Greater Palestine—Re-peopling of the Land—Jewish sources of population—Co-operation with the Moslem Arabs—The Christian Sects—Introduction of Western civilisation by the Jews—Repaying an old debt—Reform and revival of the East—The Vision of the Future . . 193–213

APPENDIX

THE REDEMPTION OF JUDÆA

SKETCHES ON THE BRITISH ADVANCE TO JERUSALEM

(1) On the Canal, and Beyond—(2) Gaza—(3) Rosetta, 1799–1917—(4) Summer-time outside Gaza—(5) The River of Gaza—(6) A Palestine Playground—(7) First days in Beersheba—(8) The "Companie" at Ludd—(9) THE REDEMPTION OF JUDÆA—(10) Jaffa Revived—(11) Jerusalem Revisited—(12) A Palestine Village at Play—(13) Passover in Jerusalem, 5678–1918 . . 215–284

MAP OF THE COLONIES . . . . *Frontispiece*

INDEX 285

PALESTINE OF THE JEWS

CHAPTER I

PALESTINE IN JEWISH HISTORY

As the Jews are the most historical of peoples so Palestine is the most historical of countries. To the whole land there may be applied the words which Cicero used of Athens: "Wherever we plant our foot we are treading on history." There is hardly a hill-top in Judæa which is not covered with the vestiges of a fortress or city of former ages, hardly a village which does not hide the site of some ancient centre of civilisation.

Here we find the stone implements of the palæolithic age illustrating the first attempt of man to conquer Nature; gigantic catacombs and Dolman areas constituting veritable prehistoric cemeteries; mounds which cover the foundations of colossal walls that encircled the fortified cities of the early Semites; ruined streets of Ionian and Corinthian columns, and the remains of vast amphitheatres and basilicas which tell of the settlement of Greeks and Romans; Byzantine churches and mosaic pavements of extraordinary thickness; stern monasteries and skeleton castles of Crusaders perched on almost inaccessible rocks—bastioned walls to-day enclosing a collection of mud huts; spacious mosques and graceful minarets soaring out of the plain; and vast stony palaces, convents and hospitals, vieing with each other in bigness and solidity, covering the hills. Cave-dwellers and Hittites, Amorites and Philistines, Hebrews and Phœnicians, Babylonians and Assyrians, Hellenes and Romans, Persians and Arabs, Franks and Saracens, Egyptians and Turks, have in turn fought for the country, and conquered it and left their traces behind them.

To humanity, therefore, Palestine is a country of peculiar interest. But for the Jews it has a surpassing importance. For nearly two thousand years it was the centre of their nation; for nearly two thousand years more it has been the centre of their hopes and aspirations. From the very beginning of their history they have regarded it with striking affection, greater and more lasting than that which any other people can have for their native land. To the Hebrews, sprung from tribes of Arab nomads and delivered from the slavery of Egypt, Canaan was the land of promise, flowing with milk and honey, the chosen place for the chosen people, "a land on which God's eyes rest from the beginning of the year to the end of the year" (Deut. xi. 12).

Israel was a nation "dwelling by itself, not counted among the peoples" (Num. xxiii. 9); and the territory of Israel likewise was set apart and aloof from the other lands, possessing unique features and "not counted among the countries." The desert isolated it on the East and South, a rocky inhospitable shore on the West cut it off from communication with the Mediterranean kingdoms, and only on the North was it at all accessible, and there the mountain ranges of Lebanon offered but narrow and difficult passes. Small as it was in extent, even when measured from Dan to Beersheba and from Carmel to beyond Jordan, it contained an extraordinary variety of climes, from the sub-tropical countries of the Jordan valley sunk hundreds of feet below the sea-level to the temperate zone of the uplands of Judæa, and from the scrubby wilderness of the Negéb to the rich pastures of Gilead. The Jewish sages, noting that the word *Ha-aretz* (Land) was used twelve times in the description of the country in Deuteronomy, taught that the land of Israel consisted of twelve different provinces, each of which constituted a country with its separate characteristics, unlike those of the others. Egypt, Mesopotamia, and Syria are lands of a single nature, and therefore they have each of them produced a people of one type. But the diversity of the different parts of Palestine fostered a striking diversity of ethnic types. Ephraim and Judah were two separate nationalities, which were held but for a short time under one sovereignty. Yet, though the influence of each part was different, the impression made by the land as a whole was extraordinarily deep.

When the division of the people of Israel had brought about the fall of either part beneath the military powers of Assyria and Babylon, and the conquerors, pursuing the policy by which they had destroyed other nationalities, tore up the people from their roots in the soil and deported them to the banks of the Tigris and the Euphrates, the love of their own land did not die out. The other conquered peoples accepted their new home and let their individuality decay; the captives of Israel and Judah wept by the river of Babylon for the country from which they were exiled, exclaiming: "If I forget thee, O Jerusalem, may my right hand forget its cunning!"

Some there were to whom the fertile plains and brilliant cities of Mesopotamia seemed more attractive than the ravaged highlands, and the ruined homesteads, from which they had been dragged. But a sturdy remnant—and in all ages it has been the remnant which has saved Israel—cheered by the prophets and taught by the scribes, nourished the hope of return till the day came when Cyrus, "the anointed of the Lord," gave the order that they should return. Then to the number of 60,000 they started on their way home, "filling their mouths with laughter, and their tongues with rejoicing" (Ps. cxxvi. 2). Led by a scion of the house of David they settled round the old centre of the nation and proceeded to rebuild there the Temple which was the outward sign of their religious supremacy. The new sanctuary was less magnificent than that of Solomon, and when it was dedicated some of those who had seen the splendour of the first wept; but it was invested with a fresh glory. It was henceforth in their eyes the religious centre not only of Israel but of the whole world, God's holy monument to which many people and mighty nations should come to seek the Lord and pray before Him (Zech. viii. 3). Their national ideal had deepened in exile and they now regarded Zion not as the seat of political grandeur but as the "City of Truth."

Judæa had a political history for the next three or four hundred years which was not distinguished. It was a tributary state, first of Persia, and then of one or other of the Hellenistic Kingdoms which had been carved out of the Persian Empire. The Jews did not aspire to State independence, they had no great military leaders, no ambitious kings. They erected no striking buildings, they created no enduring art. But Judæa had an excellence of its own. It continued to nourish a spiritual development which found expression, partly in books of religious literature, partly in a religious ordering of the life of the people. The books have been an inspiration for millions; the religious ordering of life has given the Jews a distinctive national character. The children of Israel were scattered far and wide in all the countries of Hellenistic civilisation, in Persia and Babylon, Egypt and Cyprus, the isles of Greece and the coasts of Asia Minor. "Earth and sea are full of them," said the Sibylline oracle. And at Alexandria, the intellectual capital of the world, they were gathered in hundreds of thousands and occupied two of the five quarters of the city. By their numbers and their commercial prominence they held a position there, at the centre of the Orient, analogous to that which the Jews hold in the metropolis of the New World to-day. The Alexandrians preserved their close connection with the Temple by the deputations which came up to Jerusalem at the three great festivals of the year bearing the free-will offerings of every family to the central shrine. These representatives of the Diaspora traversed desert and sea, finding the way easy because of their joy in the goal which awaited them. The pilgrimages marked outwardly the unity of the whole congregation of Israel; inwardly they secured the catholicity of the religious life.

The Maccabæan struggle which had secured the political, as well as the religious, liberty of

Judæa stimulated the spiritual consciousness of the whole nation. The teaching of the prophet that they should be " a light to the Gentiles " was now a very real inspiration. Their enthusiasm took indeed different forms in Palestine and the Diaspora ; here they became zealous for the Law, there zealous for proselytes, but everywhere proud of their special mission and their special wisdom. A new period of trial began when Palestine passed under the heel of Rome, who with her policy of blood and iron, more ruthless than that of the Babylonian conqueror, had broken the national spirit of every other people. The Jews still maintained their unyielding separateness, still obstinately preserved their ideals, and they still acted as one whole when their religion was attacked. The mad emperor Gaius (Caligula) in the first half of the first century of the Christian era sought to set up his statue in the Temple, and straightway the communities rose in the East and West so menacingly that the Roman proconsul refused to march on Palestine. Caligula was murdered before the order was carried out, but the inevitable conflict between the Kingdom of God and the kingdom of Might came to a head in the great rebellion of 66–70 C.E., which led, after five years of bitter warfare, to the ravaging of Jerusalem and the destruction of the Temple by Titus.

Palestine had been laid waste, the Jewish metropolis was no more, and on its black ruins a Roman legion was encamped. The central sanctuary had been blotted out of existence, and its most sacred vessels and the scrolls of the Law had been carried in triumph through the Forum of Rome. Millions of the land's inhabitants had been slaughtered, millions more were sold as slaves. The towns were depopulated, the villages were desolate, the fields were ravaged. It might have been expected that the communities of the Diaspora would have accepted the fall of the national centre and lost their national cohesion, remaining a separate religious body but abandoning their struggle for separate national existence. That is indeed what happened with a section of the people. The Christian heresy taught that the followers of the true faith had passed beyond their narrowness of nationalism, and the new Jerusalem in which its hopes were set was a City laid up in Heaven. But the main body held firm to the old ideals, and cherished with passionate ardour their hopes of re-establishing the Sanctuary on its old foundation. Twice they broke out in desperate revolt—in the reigns of Hadrian and Trajan—and for years they withstood the whole power of Rome. Roman legions had to be recalled from farthest Britain to put them down; but in the end the rising was crushed and an attempt was made to exterminate a people who would not be subjugated. Whole Jewish communities were wiped out in Cyprus and Cyrene, and in Palestine

PALESTINE IN JEWISH HISTORY 9

itself the country ran with blood; and on the site of Zion arose a pagan Roman city, Aelia Capitolina, from which Jews were excluded.

But though the national aspiration was defeated, the national hope was undimmed. In place of the outward visible bond of the Temple, the inner bond of the *Torah* (The Law) was strengthened. And despite massacres and pillage, Jewish life went on uninterrupted in Palestine, maintaining there its hearth of learning and of thought. Driven from Jerusalem the sages set up their schools in the smaller towns of Judæa, and when these too were destroyed, they found refuge in Galilee. The Sanhedrin, or Central Council, moved its seat ten times it was said, till at last it was located in Tiberias, the lowest city of the country, to fulfil the words of the prophet: " Thou shalt be brought very low."

Almost all the Jewish teachers of the first three centuries of the civil era came from the Holy Land; and the heads of the Palestinian schools, the Patriarchs, held almost a sovereign sway over the whole of Israel. The scattered congregations sent contributions to them, which took the place of the former offerings to the Temple services, typifying the cord of learning which united the people. Rabbi Jehudah Hanassi (the Prince) at the beginning of the third century collected and ordered the tradition in the code known as the *Mishna*, which sealed the whole development of post-

Biblical Judaism. A little more than a century later Hillel the Second, the Patriarch of Tiberias, fixed the calendar by which the calculations of the Jewish holy-days and feasts are still reckoned. There were other seats of learning in Babylon and Nehardea, in Rome and Carthage, but for long they were not deemed to compare with those in the Jewish land.

The people's deep love for the country appears over and over again in quaint Rabbinical hyperboles ; as for example when it is said : " Only he who has eaten the bread of the land of Israel knows how bread tastes " (Talmud, Tr. *Sanhedrin*) ; or again, " He who has walked four miles in the land of Israel is assured of a place in the next world " (*Ibid.*, Tr. *Kethuba*). More seriously the same feeling finds expression in the reiterated appeals in the liturgy for the rebuilding of Jerusalem and the restoration of the Temple. There is not a service nor a religious occasion in which that appeal is not voiced : morning and evening, working day, Sabbath and holiday, at marriage and death, at home and in the synagogue, the Jew from generation to generation has offered these prayers, which were originally composed by the teachers of Palestine. And time and again during the early centuries of the civil era they sought to give effect to their intense hope by rising against their foreign tyrants whenever they could ally themselves with their enemies.

The triumph of Christianity in the Roman Empire at the beginning of the fourth century inaugurated a new era of repression for the Jews. By the bitter irony of history the branch of the Jewish people which had carried part of its teaching to the heathen became the oppressors of the parent trunk, and the new missionaries of Hebrew morality waged an internecine feud with their religious rivals. The victorious sect were anxious to exclude the Jews from the place where their founder had been put to death, and to purge the land of the unfaithful who had denied him. A short-lived ray of hope was vouchsafed to the Jews during the reign of Julian the Apostate, who, hating the Christians with the hatred of a convert, looked for allies in those whom the Church itself hated. He invited the Jews to return to Jerusalem and rebuild their Temple, and they responded with alacrity. It is said that the Golden Gate of the Temple area was built by them at the time to keep out the heretics. But before the building had proceeded far Julian died; and since his day Christian Emperors have always ruled the Western world.

Persecution caused a decline of the Palestinian schools, and little by little the pre-eminence passed to Babylon, where a new "Erez Yisroel" had been settled by refugees from the West. But Babylon never commanded the affection of the Jewish people. Its schools might claim their respect for a period by reason of the authority of learning; but the heart and the soul of the people were fixed as immovably as ever on Palestine. From time to time a false Messiah would arise claiming that he would lead back the people to their land—such as Moses of Crete, who was followed by thousands into the sea. And when the Persian monarch Chosroes II sent an army to invade Palestine against the Byzantine forces (614 C.E.), thousands of Jews joined it and took part in the capture of Jerusalem. Again their victory was short-lived; for in 627 the Byzantine Emperor Heraclius marched on the city and re-took it, and he avenged the previous defeat by killing all the Jews who lived in Palestine.

Five years previously (622 C.E.) Mohammed had fled to Medina from Mecca (the event from which dates the first year of the Hejira, the Mohammedan era). In the first years of his preaching Mohammed regarded Jerusalem as the appointed centre of all true religion, and he instructed his followers to turn to the Holy Mount of Moriah in prayer. But later when he was anxious to dissociate his followers from Jewish practices, he realised that the religious centre must be changed and he altered the "Kibla" from Jerusalem to Mecca. Jerusalem however was one of the first objectives of the Mohammedan armies. The prophet himself died on the way to capture it, and in 638 the battle of the Yarmuk, one of the great engagements of the world's history, when 200,000 Christians were routed by 400,000 Arabs, left the holy city at the mercy of the Khalif. The conqueror guaranteed freedom of religious worship to all denominations, but he erected a new shrine of the new creed on the site of the Holy Temple.

The sting of persecution was relaxed from the Jews for a spell. The Cross and Crescent were struggling for the possession of the Holy Land, and the Jewish people resigned themselves to passive longing. Though no longer the centre of learning, Palestine had still a considerable Jewish population, and when the Karaites were driven from Babylon by the Rabbinist schools many of them emigrated to Jerusalem and the other towns of Jewish association, and they revived there the tradition of scholarship. The intensity of the hope which the congregations still felt towards the land of their fathers, whether in good hands or in bad, is manifest in the writings of the most brilliant of the Hebrew poets of the Golden Era of Jewish thought in Spain. Jehudah Hallevi poured forth there his songs to Zion, and finally set out on the perilous journey to the land he loved. " I am in the West, but my heart is in the East " had been his cry in Spain, and when he came to Jerusalem, and saw it in the hands of the enemies of his people, his heart broke. According to one story, he vanished in the ruins of the Temple; according to another, celebrated among the lyrics of Heine, he was pierced by an Arab's lance as he poured forth his beautiful dirges. His fate is symbolical of the hopeless love which the Jews of the Middle Ages felt for the national home.

In the twelfth century a new power had obtained sway in Palestine. The Crusaders in 1100 captured it for Christendom and divided it into a number of feudal fiefs. Jehudah Hallevi must have found Jerusalem ruled by a Latin King, and the Temple site and the Dome of the Rock occupied by the Knights Templar. The Christians were however less tolerant than the Mohammedans had been, and they had signalised the capture of Jerusalem by a butchery of the Jews. But the Jewish merchants and craftsmen had a place in the brilliant civilisation to which the meeting of East and West gave birth. At Damascus alone, the great centre of the caravans, there was a community of over 3,000 Jews. They carried their mercantile adventures to Eastern Asia and Africa, and brought the wealth of China and India, and Nubia and Abyssinia, to enrich the castles of the lords of Palestine.

Benjamin of Tudela, another Spanish Jew, who wandered over the Holy Land about 1170, describes the communities which he found at Ascalon and Tanturah, where there were skilled dyers and glass makers as well as scholars. But while the struggle between Frank and Saracen was raging, the condition of the Jewish settlers in general grew more wretched. As in feudal Europe, so in feudal Palestine, the Jew was outside the State and outside the law, and in such an atmosphere fine thinking could not flourish. Maimonides, fleeing there from the fanatical Moslems of North Africa, found no congenial resting-place, and he passed on to Egypt, where a broad-minded and liberal sovereign held sway. The prince Saladin, to whom he became physician, was a few years later to wrest Jerusalem from the Christian knights, and to bring the greater part of the country again under the sway of the Khalifs. The intervention of Maimonides was instrumental in opening the way to Palestine again to Jewish settlers, and he himself found there, after death, the desired haven which he had failed to secure in life. Jewish scholars and rabbis from France and England turned to what was again a land of promise and a land of freedom, and Jewish learning revived in Jerusalem and Tiberias. And when, at the beginning of the thirteenth century, the strolling poet, Al-Charisi, visited the land, he found everywhere flourishing communities. Intermittently, incursions by Tartar hordes spread destruction; but the settlement continued to grow. The final expulsion of the Crusaders from the coast towns occurred in 1291, synchronising with the expulsion of the Jews from England.

The land under the rule of Islam became

increasingly the refuge for the persecuted Jewish scholars of the European Ghettoes. Most distinguished of these settlers was Nachmanides, who emigrated from Spain at the age of seventy and brought to his new home the ardour for mystical speculation which marked his era. He describes the country thus: " Great is the solitude and great the waste, and the more sacred the place the greater the desolation. Jerusalem is more desolate than the rest of the country, but the fruit of the land is still magnificent and the harvest rich. It is indeed a blessed country flowing with milk and honey." The dream of the restoration though darkened by the smoke of oppression was still alive, and the hope of the Kingdom of God was translated into inner vision. Ten centuries of exile had transformed the love of Zion from an active to a contemplative feeling, and the sages in Palestine sought to hasten the advent of the Messiah by pondering on the mysteries of the world and penetrating the hidden meaning and secret wisdom of God's law. The *Kabbala* (or mystical speculation) had its origin elsewhere, but it found there its chief seat.

The expulsion of the Jews from Spain at the end of the fifteenth century brought to Palestine a new supremacy in Jewish culture. The bulk of the fugitives turned eastwards and settled in the Turkish Empire, now the dominant power of the Mohammedan world, and they introduced into the Holy Land not only the Castilian dialect (the Ladino) of the Peninsula, but something of its brilliant Hebrew culture. The land had lost its old fertility and prosperity through the repeated devastations of Tartar and Turkish hordes. Its countryside was deserted; its houses were ruined; its ports were empty; but the light of learning still shone brightly. In the new flowering of Jewish scholarship Safed, the hill city of Galilee which had been the Crusaders' stronghold, leapt into fame. It was filled with celebrated schools which exercised an authority over the whole of Jewry like that which those of its neighbour, Tiberias, had enjoyed more than a thousand years before. The Holy Spirit seemed again to have been vouchsafed to the sages of the Holy Land. And one notable attempt was made to give practical direction to the ideal of Israel's restoration. Don Joseph Nasi, descendant of a Portuguese exile, who had become the most trusted diplomatist of the Ottoman Empire and had been created Duke of Naxos, after entertaining and then abandoning the idea of establishing a Jewish colony in an island of the Greek archipelago, obtained from the Sultan, Selim II, the grant of a large tract in Galilee with the permission to rebuild the town of Tiberias and populate it exclusively with Jews. It was the anticipation of the modern movement for the return of the Jews to their ancestral soil, the first vague expression of the reviving national consciousness, and it has left its effects to this day in the settlements of Jewish agriculturists in Pekah and other villages of Northern Galilee.

The Jews of the Ottoman Empire were powerful at the time. Lady Mary Wortley Montagu writing from Constantinople at the end of the seventeenth century says of them : " These people are an incredible power in this country. They have many privileges above all the national Turks themselves, and have formed a very considerable commonwealth here, being judged by their own laws, and have drawn the whole trade of the Empire into their hands." But the Jewish people as a whole was not ready yet for a large movement of repatriation. The influences of the Ghetto had crippled the wings of its imagination, and at the same time impaired its power of action. Under the leadership of the pseudo-Messiah, Sabbatai Zevi, the Eastern Jews indeed rose in their thousands to inaugurate a new Kingdom of God in the Holy Land. Two of his chief supporters are described as " Nathan of Gaza " and " Joseph of Ascalon," proving that Jewish congregations still flourished in the ancient cities of Palestine. But with the downfall of its leader the movement collapsed even more quickly than it had sprung up. Its followers were looking rather for a sudden miraculous intervention than for the continuous aid of Providence, which manifests itself through the

PALESTINE IN JEWISH HISTORY 19

earnest efforts of men. And the effect of their hopeless enterprise was only to sap for generations the vigour of Oriental Jewry, and to bring about the secession of a sect who continued to believe in the pseudo-Messiah. Their descendants to this day, the Donmeh, are strong in what was European Turkey and had their chief seat in Salonica. The belief in a sudden Divine intervention led the Millenarian Christians of England to co-operate with Manasseh ben Israel in procuring, in Cromwell's time, the re-settlement of the Jews in England, which they regarded as a preliminary of the national return to Palestine. At the same time the colonisation of the New World led to several striking proposals to gather the outcasts of Israel in a new home. The Dutch East India Company suggested a new Zion in Curaçoa; the famous French General, Marshal Saxe, looked to South America; but these schemes never passed the stage of design.

In Palestine itself the decay of the Jewish communities set in as the government of the Turks weakened and left the country a prey to the wild roving tribes of Bedouins. But Israel is never altogether deserted; the undying love of the people for their land received a new outlet when the famous Rabbi Elijah, known as the Gaon of Wilna, at the end of the eighteenth century, revived in the form of the *Chalukah* the old contribution to the Jewish schools of the holy cities. His aim was to preserve a centre of Jewish learning in the place of Israel's hopes, and his project was received with enthusiasm throughout Russia and Poland, Galicia and Germany, Hungary and Holland. Some hundreds of scholars settled in the Holy Cities. In recent times the Chalukah system has been abused, but for years it had the merit of maintaining a remnant in the land, and of giving a concrete form to the spiritual yearning of the people.

The hope of the return had for seventeen centuries never been dried up and never became outworn. It had given to the harried, hunted and persecuted Jewish people, driven from land to land, denied in places even human rights, nowhere at home, nowhere accepted into civil society, the vision without which it must have perished. It had lived in their imagination, endowed with an ideal life in their prayers and their religious observances, called to mind on every occasion of joy or sorrow. It had been the magnetic lodestar by which the ship of Jewish Nationalism, often rudderless and often without any captain, had held on its course. And if the hope of the physical return had, in the blurring process of time, become dimmer, this ideal of the Yishub (the "return" of the nation) had always remained to illumine the obscurity of the Ghetto, and to give a meaning to Jewish suffering.

CHAPTER II

THE MODERN ZIONIST MOVEMENT

THE French Revolution, which heralded a new era for humanity, ushered in also a new era for the Jew. In France, in Germany, and in England, under the influence of liberal ideas and the belief in the rights of Man, the gates of the Ghetto were broken down; in the United States of America, where, from the time of the Declaration of Independence, the idea of human equality was accepted as an integral part of the polity, the gates were never erected: and in these countries, though the clouds of prejudice might still hover, it was possible for the Jew to become a freeman and a citizen of the world. The genius which had been cribbed, cabined and confined for generations, wasted if it could not find scope in the preservation of Judaism, burst forth to display itself in a more spacious field. While the Gentile peoples were proclaiming Liberty, Equality and Fraternity, from among the Jews a cry was raised "Out of the tribal, into the human." That was the idea implicit in the Mendelssohnian "enlightenment," and it guided the Paris Sanhedrin of 1796 which sealed the Concordat between the Jews of France and the French Republic.

The Jews were to give up their particular national institutions and their particular national aspirations, and to become full members of the French nation, distinguished from other Frenchmen only by certain religious beliefs and practices. Judaism, like Catholicism, or Protestantism, was to be reduced to a matter of creed; and the Jews were to find their whole national life in the countries where they dwelt. While the other European peoples were reviving their dormant sense of nationality, which had been crushed for centuries by the influence of the Holy Roman Empire, the Jews, who in spite of repression, persecution and world-wide dispersal had for centuries retained a consciousness of nationality, sought to denationalise themselves! In the ancient world they had been national when all others were cosmopolitan: now they became cosmopolitan when all others were national. Their attitude was like that of the mad Hercules who, having performed his heroic labours, returned to his house and killed his own children. It is not difficult to understand what induced this change of outlook. Civil and political emancipation appeared to be the one boon necessary; and the price of it, at the time, was a declaration of national suicide.

It is noteworthy however that Napoleon, who, as First Consul, pressed for the Concordat of Jewry with the French State, on invading Egypt and Syria in 1799 realised the undying appeal of Palestine, and issued an invitation to the Jews of Asia and Africa to settle again under his ægis in Jerusalem. He published a political manifesto to this end in the *Moniteur Universelle* (No. 243). But his attempt to be the modern Cyrus had even less fruition than the attempt of the Emperor Julian 1,500 years previously. His Eastern campaign collapsed before Acre, and Palestine remained under the misgovernment of the Turks.

Within a short time, indeed, Palestine was conquered by Ibrahim the son of Mehemet Ali, the Pasha of Egypt, who had made himself Sultan. Under his strong rule there was a promise of better things. When Sir Moses Montefiore paid his first visit to the Holy Land in 1827 he met Ibrahim and negotiated with him as to the Jewish colonisation of the deserted plains and villages of the country. The noble-hearted Jewish philanthropist entertained, in common with the best of the emancipated Jews of the time, a profound feeling, in idealised form, for the country of Israel's past, which found expression with him in the effort to re-establish there a Jewish Commonwealth. Jerusalem was inscribed on his coat of arms, and the desire of his heart was to see Palestine again fertile, and again peopled by Jews. But before his plan of colonisation could be started Mehemet Ali had been compelled by the European Powers to renounce his sway over Syria and to restore the country to Turkey. With the Turks there was at the time no chance of negotiation, and Sir Moses Montefiore had to restrict his efforts to the betterment of the conditions of the few thousand Jews who were already living in the country. One is fain to reflect how different the history of Palestine during the last century might have been if it had remained in the dominion of the Pasha of Egypt, and had passed, with the rest of his dominions, under the control of England in the " eighties."

English Christians as well as English Jews cherished the idea of Jewish re-settlement in the Holy Land as a step towards the fulfilment of prophecy; and in 1846 Colonel George Gawler sent to the Queen and to the leading men of the country, a book entitled *The Tranquillisation of Syria and the East by the Establishment of Jewish Colonies in Palestine*. Similar in tendency was the work of Hollingsworth, who in his *Jews in Palestine* (1852) urged the re-establishment of a Jewish State under British protection as a means of securing the overland route to India. In 1854 a " Palestine Land Company " was provisionally registered in England with the object of raising a fund by shares for the purpose of enabling the descendants of Israel to settle on the land. The promoters believed that 100,000 pioneers were ready at a moment's notice to avail themselves of the first safe opportunity that offered for their restoration to the land of their ancestors.

The Crimean War, which arose immediately out of the trouble between rival churches as to the custody of the Holy Places in Jerusalem, directed the attention of the Great Powers, and the outbreak at the same period of the Blood Accusation at Damascus—which led to a brutal attack on the Jewish quarter—directed anew the attention of the emancipated Jewish communities, towards Palestine. The Christian Churches began to vie with each other in providing religious institutions on the sites secured by them in Jerusalem, and the Jewish communities of the West founded schools and hospitals and other philanthropic institutions for their brethren in various parts of the country. But in the latter half of the century a more radical change in the outlook of the Jews towards Palestine, the transformation of the idea of the Restoration to Zion from the region of dreams to the region of reality, was brought about by an intensification of the national feeling of Europe, and a revival of their own national consciousness.

As the permanent influences of the French Revolution worked themselves out, the idea of the rights of Man was amplified by the idea of the rights of nationalities. It was claimed that every aggregation of men conscious of forming a separate nationality, whether united by language or tradition or history, or all these, should be an autonomous nation ; and in the light of this principle Greece, Belgium, and Italy, and later the Balkan and Scandinavian peoples, asserted and established their political independence. At the same time in the gradual decline of the respect for the rights of Man by themselves, the old feelings of dislike and contempt for the Jew, fanned by inherited prejudice or bureaucratic machinations, began to get the upper hand in the less enlightened parts of Europe. In Germany and Austria his hardly won emancipation was soon hedged in and circumscribed ; in Russia, where the great mass of the Jewish population still live, civil emancipation was never won. The progressive spirit of the age combined with the reaction of the time to revive the Jewish feeling of nationality, and to shatter the shallow philosophy of the early leaders of the " enlightenment " movement, who had sought by denial of any national individuality to smooth the way for the absorption of the Jews into the European polity.

It was in the *Rome and Jerusalem* of a German Socialist, Moses Hess, published in 1860, that the revival which had been generated by these external facts obtained its first clear literary expression. As the title of his work suggested, Hess saw in the liberation of Italy the prelude to the re-birth of the Jewish nation. " With the freeing of the Eternal City on the Tiber began that of the Eternal City on Mount Moriah: with the renaissance of Italy the resurrection of Judæa." Thought, as usual, was someway ahead of action, but this idea of Israel's resurrection in the land of his fathers began to spread, and then to be translated into deeds. It found beautiful utterance in one of the great English writers of the century. George Eliot made it the pivot of her novel *Daniel Deronda*, and put into the mouth of one of her ideal creations, Mordecai, the prophecy of a new Judæa poised between East and West to be a covenant of reconciliation: " The Jew will claim the brotherhood of his own nation, and carry it into a new brotherhood with the nations of the Gentiles." Dean Stanley, also, in his book on Palestine wrote of the possibility that " in the changes of the Turkish Empire the Jewish race, so wonderfully preserved, may yet have another stage of national existence opened to them ; they may once more obtain possession of their native land, and invest it with an interest greater than it could have under any other circumstances."

The two most brilliant men of action in emancipated Jewry dreamed in their youth of leading back their people to their old land. Benjamin Disraeli declared that *Alroy*, the romance of the Jewish mediæval hero who claimed to be the Messiah, and inaugurated his work by conquering Palestine, portrayed his ideal ambition. And in *Tancred*, a work of greater maturity, where the scene is laid in Palestine, the Jewish heroine exclaims: " The race that persists in celebrating the vintage, although it has no fruit to gather, will in time regain its vineyards." Ferdinand Lassalle, about the same time as Disraeli was composing *Alroy*, wrote in his diary: " I love to picture myself sword in hand leading back the tribes of Israel to their home." Both were diverted from the ideal ambitions of their youth to other courses, because in their day there seemed to be no Jewish movement to lead. Yet one of the sanest organs of English public opinion, *The Spectator*, declared, " If Lord Beaconsfield [at the Congress of Berlin] had freed the Holy Land and restored the Jews, instead of pottering about with Roumelia and Afghanistan, he would have died Dictator."

The stimulus which roused into activity the latent love of the Jewish masses for Palestine was the recrudescence of a violent persecution in Russia in 1881. The Ghetto had not been broken down in Eastern Europe, and the historic consciousness of the Jews was far stronger there than in the emancipated West. Already societies of the " Lovers of Zion" (*Chovevi Zion*) had begun to establish little agricultural settlements which were planting vineyards on the ruined terraces of Judæa and reclaiming to fertility the plains of Philistia. Already a Jewish Agricultural School had been founded by the Alliance Israélite Universelle outside Jaffa to prepare the way for larger and systematic colonisation. And already the brilliant English man of letters and erratic man of State affairs, Laurence Oliphant, had begun to negotiate with the Sultan of Turkey for the re-population of the land of Gilead on the East side of Palestine with thousands of sturdy Jewish agriculturalists. While in the West the chief energies of the leaders were directed towards the completion of political emancipation, the love of Zion asserted itself in the Ghettoes of Eastern Europe. There the religious enthusiasm of the Rabbi Kalischer moved those whom the more philosophical eloquence of Hess had failed to touch. Where circumstances were at their lowest the will to enlargement was strongest.

The idealist movement " Back to the Land " had begun before persecution came to spur it: but the relapse of Russia into mediæval barbarism, which threatened the destruction or demoralisation of six million Jews, brought it home anew to the whole of Jewry that in the words of their daily prayer : " God hath not made us like the nations of other lands and hath not placed us like other families of the earth." It was recognised that the people must be got out of the Russian inferno, and a new exodus began which has carried every year something like 150,000 souls to new homes. True that the main tide of emigration has flowed to the New World ; true that one million Jews, the greatest aggregation in Jewish annals since the destruction of the Temple, were gathered in New York; true that Baron de Hirsch, who devoted his millions to the furtherance of Jewish agricultural colonisation, looked for a new land of Israel in the Argentine Republic, and that the corporation to which he bequeathed his vast fund continued to prefer any corner of the world to Palestine; true that many Jewish philanthropists and some dreamers of the Ghetto, feverishly anxious to find a refuge for the masses of emigrants where they may live a free life according to their traditions have searched, in vain, for Jewish territories in every continent; yet Palestine has become year by year the common goal of the Jewish people and its most living ideal.

To those who are eager to secure a permanent home for Judaism as well as a refuge for the Jew, where the soul as well as the body of Jewry might be invigorated, Palestine has remained the only possible goal. And within the last thirty years the movement "Back to the Land" has gone on steadily, and the Jewish population has increased manifold. It numbered barely 10,000 in 1830 and less than 20,000 fifty years later, in 1880. On the outbreak of the war of 1914 it amounted to about 120,000. When the American scholar, Robinson, visited Jerusalem in the year 1828 he estimated that of the 11,000 inhabitants 3,000 were Jews, and in 1825 another traveller,

Dickson, laughed at the idea of 6,000 Jews in the place thriving on the wants of 40,000 Arabs and Greeks. In 1914, before the war broke out, there were over 60,000 Jews in the Holy City out of a total population of 100,000.

Sir Moses Montefiore found a bare *Minyan* (ten) of Jews at Jaffa when he landed there on the first of his various pilgrimages (1827). At the outbreak of the war the town numbered 20,000 Jews, a third of its population, and its most active and popular element. Twenty years ago there existed no Jewish congregation at Haifa, the natural harbour of the country; now a community of between two and three thousand souls flourishes there, and Jews have played a great part in the development of the commerce, and Jewish educational institutions are springing up in its suburbs. In the country, as well as in the towns, the seeds of the new Jewish life have been planted. The taunt which Cobbett levelled at the Jewish people that "like the voracious slug they live on the things produced by others and produce nothing themselves," has gradually been refuted. Before the outbreak of the war some forty Jewish villages or settlements had been founded in all parts of the country with a total population of over 12,000. By the work of Jewish hands the plain of Sharon was again made fruitful with vineyards, and the uplands of Galilee with cornfields; the hills of Judæa were again terraced with olives, and orchards were planted again in the Valley of the Jordan.

The Jewish settlements, it is true, are small and are so far miniatures of what is to be accomplished; in their totality they cover not much more than two per cent of the soil of Palestine. But their influence has already been marked in the trade and industry of the country. A British Blue Book published by the Board of Trade in 1911 stated that the chief feature in the economic development of Southern Syria was the Jewish immigration: and the growth of the trade of Jaffa in the decade preceding the Balkan war (which brought a temporary check) is eloquent of the stimulating effect on Oriental indolence of Jewish enterprise. In 1900 the value of the exports passing through the Port was £264,000, in 1911 it rose to £682,000, and the value of the imports rose during the same period from £380,000 to over one million sterling. The growth in the export of oranges from Jaffa since the Jewish immigration began is typical of the progress; in 1883 50,000 cases were exported; in 1913 two million cases.

The increase of the Jewish population did not come altogether from the West, but was gathered literally from the four corners of the Exile. Palestine is the lodestar of every Jewish community, and little bands make their way continually from the congregations of the larger Eastern centres—Bagdad, Aleppo and

Bokhara; from Arabia and Persia, Morocco and Turkestan; even from India and Abyssinia. Jerusalem in particular is a microcosm of scattered Jewry. The chief source of the new population is naturally Russia, which is followed by Roumania and Galicia. The largest Oriental immigration is from the Yemen district, in which the Jews have been settled since the destruction of the Kingdom. There they have lived as serfs for ages, oppressed by the fanatical Moslem Arabs around them but cherishing the more intensely the hope of returning to the home of their ancestors. Twenty years ago small parties of these Yemenites made their way to Palestine, and finding there the chance of a better life and freedom, they have brought over several thousands of their community. They are very industrious and patient, less intellectual than the Western Jews, but not so restless, and they have provided a very valuable labour force both in the towns and in the fields.

The gentle stream of Jewish immigration back to the country, and the gradual trickling of that immigration back to the soil, preceded and fostered the growth of a conscious national movement for making Palestine again the home of the Jewish people. It was not till the nineteenth century had nearly run its course, in 1897, that a Viennese playwright and littérateur, Theodor Herzl, stung to full Jewish consciousness himself by the shame of the Dreyfus case, called a congress of Jewish representative men at Basle in Switzerland and founded our latter-day Zionism. The aim of the movement was defined as " the establishment in Palestine of a publicly - secured and legally - guaranteed Home for the Jewish people "; the immediate objective was to obtain a charter from the Sultan, backed by the Great Powers, for autonomous Jewish colonisation in the Holy Land; and the means to that end were, first the rousing and strengthening of the Jewish national feeling in every Jewish community, and the organisation of the Jewish people internationally for combined action, and secondly the establishment of a national Trust, in the form of a banking company, for the purchase of land and the work of colonisation. Herzl's call converted the sleeping sentiment of the masses into an ardent enthusiasm: the efforts of the few pioneers into a national striving. The literary artist became the statesman; and for the first time for centuries the Jewish people had a hero of action, who devoted himself entirely to their cause. Herzl found his largest following first in the Jewish proletariat of Eastern Europe and the East End of London, and secondly among the Jewish students of the Universities. He was at once joined by several of the Jewish intellectual leaders, among them Max Nordau and Barnard Lazare, the Champion of Dreyfus, in France, and Israel Zangwill in

MODERN ZIONIST MOVEMENT 35

England. But he was almost immediately opposed and savagely attacked by the communal leaders in Western Europe, who regarded his cry as a menace to the tranquil enjoyment of the political and civil emancipation which the preceding generation had won.

It is not the place here to discuss the development of the Zionist movement and its varying fortunes; we have to consider only its effect on Jewish life in Palestine. The immediate objective of a Charter for Jewish colonisation was not attained, though Herzl by his personal magnetism and diplomatic genius was able to secure the support of several of the monarchs and chancelleries of Europe. But the "financial instrument" was established as an English Company—the Jewish Colonial Trust—with a nominal capital of two millions, towards which a quarter of a million was subscribed in the first year. In addition a "Jewish National Fund" was incorporated, also in England, to acquire land for public purposes as a kind of national domain. In the year before the war this Fund had received over £200,000, and the subscriptions for the year reached a million francs, or £40,000. It had begun on a small scale to accomplish its purpose of creating a national domain in country villages and towns, starting afforestation with olive groves on the spurs of the Judæan hills, establishing training farms and workmen's dwellings in Judæa and Galilee, and providing sites for the Hebrew schools and the higher educational institutions of Jerusalem, Jaffa and Haifa.

Herzl was opposed at first to the support of the small colonising enterprises which had been started during the preceding twenty years by the "Lovers of Zion"; he wanted the Jews to come in by the open door, in a large body, and not to slink in by little groups. The little, he thought, was the enemy of the big. But when the hope of the Charter was disappointed, he recognised the necessity of organising and developing the Jewish life in the country and giving it a more independent and representative character than it yet possessed. If the immigration of hundreds of thousands was impossible for the time, at least the thousands who entered and the thousands who were there could live under the conditions which were desired for the whole people when the larger measures could be undertaken. To further the expansion of trade and the development of agricultural colonies, a branch of the Jewish Colonial Trust, the Anglo-Palestine Bank, was founded with a paid-up capital of £100,000, and at the outbreak of the war this Zionist Bank had become one of the chief financial institutions in Southern Syria; the deposits amounted to £250,000, and its total operations for the year 1913 rose to five million pounds sterling.

In the waiting period Herzl sought to plant a Jewish colony in the vestibule of Palestine which was within the boundaries of Egypt. England was of all the Powers the most sympathetic to Jewish aspirations; and he had a passionate enthusiasm for her liberal governing spirit. Checked in his hopes at Constantinople he asked for the support of England's great pro-consul in Egypt, for a scheme of colonising the district of El-Arish between the Sinai desert and the Turkish frontier. It was a region inhabited then very sparsely and roughly cultivated by Bedouin Arabs, but which has since become better known by the advance of the British armies in 1917 through this vestibule to Palestine. The Government at home countenanced the idea, and a Commission went out from England to survey the land. But, without extended irrigation, settlement on anything like a considerable scale did not appear feasible; and at the time the controlling authorities in Egypt did not recommend the grant of irrigation facilities from Egypt's perennial stream. The project, therefore, was dropped. But in its place the Colonial Office, then under the guidance of Mr. Joseph Chamberlain, who had been attracted by the magnetic personality of the Jewish leader, put forward a proposal for an autonomous Jewish settlement in British East Africa. Herzl welcomed this signal recognition of Jewish hopes, but the Zionist rank and file, when the proposal was brought forward very dramatically, without previous notice, at the

Congress of 1905 were gravely divided upon it. A section, consisting mainly of Jews of Western Europe, were enthusiastically in favour of pursuing the offer and sending a Commission to investigate the territory; another section, consisting of the "Lovers of Zion" and the Jews of Eastern Europe, who were the principal strength of the existing Palestinian settlement, were for rejecting it out of hand. Though grateful for England's unlooked-for intervention, their ideal was indissolubly bound up with their historic home, and no other land, though graced with every liberty, could take its place in their affections. Herzl by force of leadership prevailed on the assembly to send out the Commission for enquiry and report to a future Congress. But shortly after he broke down and died, leaving to his people a double treasure, the priceless heritage of a living ideal and the immortal memory of a dead hero.

After Herzl's death the cleavage in the ranks induced by the Uganda project became pronounced, and a small section, under the leadership of Zangwill, split off from the main body and formed the Jewish Territorial Organisation (the I.T.O.). Ever since that time this Organisation has chased, from continent to continent, the will of the wisp of an autonomous Jewish settlement outside Palestine, and found no resting-place. The Commission that went to Uganda reported unfavourably on the area which was in the end proffered. The I.T.O. looked to Tripoli, which was still under the Ottoman sway, and sent another Commission, which also reported adversely. As it was put by the President of the Organisation himself, that scheme would "not hold water." Then the gaze was directed towards another part of the Ottoman Empire; Mesopotamia was held out as the Land of Promise. The report as to the possibilities here was more brilliant, and the land had abundant Jewish associations, but nothing came of the proposal except another series of scintillating speeches from the erratic I.T.O. leader. The later ventures of the I.T.O. quest were less happy in conception, and no more fruitful in result. Angola, Nicaragua, Westralia, were looked at in vain; and finally the grand project of a Jewish autonomous territory petered out in a movement for the diffusion of Jewish emigration in the United States. To-day the remnant of Territorialists are ready to merge with the Zionists in the choice of Palestine as the Jewish land.

A more radical opposition to the Palestine movement has been maintained by the more prosperous section of Jewry, especially in the countries where Jews have been politically emancipated. They have harked back to the declaration of the leaders in the struggle for that emancipation and have repudiated, in whole or in part, the existence of a Jewish nationality, or the desire of the Jews to become again a nation. They form three main classes; those who admit that the Jews are a spiritual nationality but assert that it is a retrograde step to attempt to restore the Jewish country and rebuild the Jewish home; those who claim that Judaism is purely a religion and the Jews only members of a religious creed; and those who profess a belief in the ultimate Jewish restoration to Palestine, but regard human effort to bring about that restoration as impiety. Of all three classes it may be said generally that they look on the Jewish past without perspective, on its present without a policy, and on its future without faith.

Many of those who opposed the efforts to re-establish the Jewish people in Palestine admitted a special Jewish interest in the country of their ancestors. They were prepared to encourage settlements on the land and the foundation of schools: but there must be no suggestion of a separate political nationality. Not a few who had supported Palestinian colonisation in the days preceding Herzl's advent were perturbed by his larger and more radical appeal, which they feared would imperil their adopted citizenship. The iron of the Ghetto bars and bolts had entered into their souls, and survived the destruction of the Ghetto walls. Emancipated and received as equals in civil life, these Jews of the

West could not feel secure, and they feared that their rights might be taken from them if they asserted their true character and stood fearless before the world as members of a nationality that had its special territory elsewhere and developed its special way of life. In one of his speeches advocating an "Itoland" Zangwill told the story of a celebrated French painter who wishing to paint an old beggar could find no model that satisfied him till, one day, dining with a wealthy Jew he suddenly said to his host: "Will you sit for me? I have been searching in vain for a model of a beggar, and you are the only man who looks the part." The simile may be bitter but it is true that, though outwardly free, the assimilated Jew was often inwardly a slave. He was prepared to support the colonies and institutions in Palestine so long as they wore a philanthropic guise; he turned in dismay from the vision of a Palestine regenerated and independent, a Jewish country inhabited by a people grown to self-consciousness, speaking a revived Hebrew tongue, and living according to the old Hebraic ideal. Might not their neighbours cast it in their teeth that they should go there too? And would not a Jewish country be a larger Ghetto painfully inferior to the spacious empires in which their lot was cast? The return to Palestine was, they said, a surrender to the anti-Semites, and Zionism was only a feeble reaction to anti-Semitism.

Spinoza foresaw three centuries ago that Jewish individuality must be threatened when emancipation passed from the political to the social sphere, and the Jewish development in the latter half of the nineteenth century proved him correct. Zionism has its roots, not as its opponents say in anti-Semitism, but rather in the resistance to assimilation. It does not indeed challenge one of the premisses of anti-Semitism, that the Jews are " a people among the peoples, and a nation among the nations." It accepts this, because it is true; but it claims that the members of a national, as of a religious community, may still enjoy, everywhere, full civil and political rights, though they may have elsewhere some national centre. It expresses the desire of the sturdy remnant to preserve the Jewish spirit which has been imperilled in prosperity. A Homeland will but focus the Jewish people and Jewish thought.

The position of those who claimed that Judaism was purely a religion, and the Jews merely members of a religious creed, was equally unstable. It is the outstanding characteristic of Judaism that religion and nationality have, from the beginning, been inextricably combined. The struggle with Christianity in the early centuries of the civil era turned largely on the Jewish refusal to sever them. Nor can the severance be made now without cutting off the source of life.

The Jews, in their lackland and non-political condition, have carried about with them for centuries a moral Palestine, which has bound them together and preserved from death their ideals and their individuality. To-day, when they enjoy civil and political rights, and are no longer living in a cramped concentration, they need a visible Palestine to endow their ideals with fresh life, and to secure a common point of unity. A persecuted segregated nationality may survive through outward oppression; an emancipated and dispersed nationality can flourish as a distinct force only if it possesses some inward source of vitality; and that it can gain only from a hearth of its own.

The talk of a Jewish mission, to be achieved by dispersion among the nations, which would be frustrated by a Jewish concentration in Palestine, is vague and hollow. The champions of this view can point to no missionaries; and, while basing themselves on the prophecy that the people of Israel should be "a light to the nations," they disregard the primary fact that the prophets contemplated a Jewish people returned to its land, sending its emissaries to the four corners of the earth. The re-establishment of the centre was an essential part of the prophets' dream, and it is an essential condition of any revival of Jewish spiritual influence among the nations of to-day. As the rabbis expressed it, " God will not come to the heavenly Jerusalem till Israel has returned to the earthly Jerusalem." Without a living centre there can be no radiating influence. For those who believe sincerely in the Jewish mission the return to Palestine must be the first object of endeavour; otherwise their hope is, in the words of a mediæval Hebrew poet and lover of Zion, but " as the twittering of sparrows."

With those who profess to believe in a Jewish restoration in Palestine, but regard human effort to achieve it as impious, it is harder to reason. Their position is so mediæval that it is proof against argument. The spirit of the age is against them. All enlightened men and women to-day would accept the proverbial philosophy about " those whom God helps," or the saying of Florence Nightingale, " God builds His finest bridges with men, and not angels, for His pillars." And if a Jewish people living in Palestine is a good ideal, then it must be for the living, the Jews of to-day, to work with all their might for its accomplishment. Perhaps the guidance of Providence in the present world-war may appear manifest enough to these latter-day pietists and make them realise that by work, as well as by prayer, they may speed the coming of the Messianic age. The outward events of the struggle, as well as the fundamental principles underlying it, have cut the ground from under the feet of the anti-Zionists.

In the earlier half of the nineteenth century

men cherished vague aspirations for a colourless cosmopolitanism which gave way in the second half of the century to a burning passion for an intense nationalism. The twentieth century is developing to fruitfulness, through terrible birth agonies, the idea of a harmonious internationalism composed of democratic nation-communities, equal in right though not all sovereign, freely exchanging ideas and products, and contributing loyally to the welfare of the whole. In that society the twelve millions of Jews have their great part to play. They are the most perfectly dispersed, and at the same time the most consciously distinctive, of peoples; but to play their part, without wearing the badge of sufferance, they must have, like every other national unit, their own national centre in which those will live who are anxious to create afresh a conscious Hebraism.

Before the flood of the war the tide had been flowing strongly towards Zionism. Among the young generation especially, and the men and the women under the age of twenty-five on whom the future of a people depends, the recognition of Jewish nationality and the need of rebuilding a Jewish national home, if Judaism was to be a constructive force, was continually growing in strength. Not only in Eastern and Central Europe, where the sting of political persecution and social ostracism was added, but in France and Italy,

England and the British Dominions and America, where Jews took their full part in the life of the country, at almost every University attended by a considerable number of Jewish students, a Zionist society sprang into being. The proletariat and the intellectuals remained the two main elements of the active Zionist body; but the sentiment for Palestine began to spread throughout the circles of the bourgeoisie and the ruling families. It was partly the influence of Palestinian achievement, partly the working of the young idea, that brought about this change of view.

In the year preceding the outbreak of war a remarkable number of leaders in Jewry visited the Holy Land, among them Baron Edmond de Rothschild, the veteran Lord Bountiful of the Colonies, and Mr. Henry Morgenthau, then the Ambassador to Turkey of the United States. Baron Edmond was moved to tears by the joy he experienced over the living Hebrew tongue which he met wherever he went. The pilgrimage was coming to be regarded as a necessary qualification for Zionist leadership, and usually made or converted a sympathiser into an enthusiast. The effect which the sight of the budding Jewish life had on those willing to seek it is illustrated by some remarks made by Mr. Morgenthau in an interview after his return. "Everywhere," he said, "I encountered proud, free and contented beings; there was nothing of a sense of oppression, no trace of bent backs, and of those furtive glances which are characteristic of Jews who have to endure persecution, the sad product of centuries of Ghetto life. Men stood before me who were not wanting in self-consciousness and self-respect, men who believed in themselves and in their future. I saw there too, women and girls at work in the fields and the gardens, and also amusing themselves by dancing. It was hardly believable that these were the same wómen and girls who, only a brief while ago, worked with bent frames at the sewing machine, or were students who industriously pored over books. Instinctively I thought of the freed bird which, as soon as it emerges from its narrow cage, soars into the pure air of the woods and fields and bursts into joyous song."

Thirty years of pioneer work had made the Yishub already a pride and inspiration to the whole of Jewry. And during the war the sentiment has hardened into a conviction that the opportunity for the Jewish restoration has come. In every part of the world the Jewish democracy is demanding that at the end of the war Palestine shall be a Jewish country, and every democracy in the world supports their demand. It found its consecration in the Declaration of the British Government on November 2nd, 1917, which will for ever be a red-letter day in Jewish history, proclaiming that England views with sympathy the Zionist effort towards the establishment of a Jewish national home in Palestine, and pledges its best endeavours to the securing of that object.

At the Congress of Vienna in 1815, with which the war era of the French Revolution at last came to an end, the Jewish representatives who hovered on the outskirts of the gathering were concerned to secure for the Jewish communities of Central Europe, what the communities of France had already secured—civil and political rights. They wanted Jews to be counted of the nation, but not as a nation. At the Congress which will follow the war of our own era the representatives of the Jews, admitted it may be hoped as the spokesmen of a nationality, will ask of the assembled Powers that their claims to return to their historic home as a people may be granted in order that they may make the land again a fruitful centre, fruitful with the products of nature and fruitful also with the products of human life: "Joy and gladness shall be found in it, song and the sound of mirth."

CHAPTER III

THE AGRICULTURAL COLONIES

1. JUDÆA

"The nation, in every country," said John Bright, "dwells in the cottage." Common origin, common history, common language, common religion, common ideals, these are all elements of nationality: but they only combine to produce the fine flower of a nation when the people which possesses them is rooted in a soil. For it is by contact with the land, by long association with certain scenes and sights, and by continual intercourse with Nature in all her moods in a particular country, that the character of a folk is called out. A people may preserve its individuality, and keep alive its spiritual heritage, though divorced from the soil. But it cannot in that condition attain the higher pinnacles of creative thought. It will live, but not live well. For nigh two thousand years the Jews, dispersed over the habitable globe, have maintained their national existence: but since the Roman Emperors and Christian Bishops exiled them from Palestine they have not added fresh treasures to the world's thought worthy of the Nation which gave to humanity the prophets of Judæa, the Psalmists, the writers of the Wisdom literature, or the religious Reformers of the first and second centuries. The uprooting from the land has meant the decay of the Jewish genius, so that the Jew to-day in the eyes of the mass of mankind is a type of commercial success. Circumstances have forced their genius into less worthy channels; regeneration must proceed from the soil. Palestine cannot be the centre of a living Jewish culture until it is also a land cultivated by a Jewish population, settled in their own homesteads, and earning their bread by the sweat of their brow.

The prophets of the first Exile pictured the return as bringing a revival of fertility to the land of Israel: " God will make the wilderness of Judæa as Eden, and her dry places as the garden of the Lord." " Every man shall sit beneath his vine and beneath his fig-tree." And these pictures of the restoration have been instilled into the minds of every generation of the people in the long dispersion which has forced them first from the soil of their own land and then from the soil altogether, and driven them into congested " Jewish quarters," where they have been cut off from the beauties of God's earth. The ideal which they have cherished finds simple expression in the prayer of the Eve of Passover, marking the culmination of the service of the Festival of Freedom, in which thanks are given " for the vine and for the fruit of the vine, for the produce of the field and for the desirable and goodly and ample land which thou wast pleased to grant as an heritage to our ancestors that they might eat of its fruits and be sated with its bounties," as they yearn to be. The love of Nature has been preserved, not only in this but in each of the great festivals of the Jewish year. Passover is the feast of the barley harvest : Pentecost of the first-fruits : Tabernacles of the ingathering of the vintage. A national holiday, observed in the Ghetto, though almost forgotten by emancipated Jewry, marks the day on which the trees begin to put forth their leaf in Palestine after the winter's cold. This " New Year of the Trees," which falls in February, is a kind of Jewish May-day. It has a certain pathos, also, that at the Passover and Tabernacle festivals the ritual contains special prayers for dew and rain. Everywhere throughout the Diaspora, the Jew still utters, in their due season, the prayers for the moisture and the showers that mean so much to Palestine.

There is a widespread notion that Jews have an inveterate distaste and an inherent incapacity for agricultural life, and that they turn, everywhere, of their free choice, to commerce and industry and the liberal professions. It is indeed generally recognised that, as long as Palestine was the national centre, they were essentially an agricultural and pastoral people.

The evidence of the Bible is too clear upon the point to be gainsaid; and it requires the imperturbable ingenuity of the anti-Semitic German professors to find signs of their predestined commercial development and their huckstering nature in the Scriptures. It is not, however, so generally known that for centuries after the return from Babylon, indeed so long as they were permitted to dwell in their own country, the Jews remained in heart and in deed attached to the soil. The settled life on the land was always their ideal of happiness, whether contrasted with the nomad life of those who trafficked in caravans over the desert or the limited freedom of the artisan's bench and the merchant's counting-house.

Josephus explains the silence of the classical Greek historians about his people by the fact that they did not engage in trade, as did the Phœnicians or the Egyptians. "We neither inhabit the maritime country, nor do we delight in merchandise: but having a fruitful country for our habitation, we devote ourselves to its cultivation." The brutal devastation of their land by the Roman legions, and the attempt to drive them from their homes which followed on the struggle against Titus, and the still more desperate outbreak against Hadrian, could not destroy their love of the soil. Excluded from Judæa they founded new homesteads in Galilee and in Babylon. The rabbis of the early centuries of the civil era are never weary of drawing homilies in praise of the pursuit of agriculture. From the verse in the Psalms: "The Heavens are the heavens of the Lord, but the Earth hath He given to the sons of men," one of the sages taught that " he who owns no land is no man." Another interpreted the saying in Proverbs: "He who works his ground shall be satisfied with bread," to mean that if a man works as a labourer on the soil he shall gain his sustenance, and if he does not he shall go unsatisfied. "He that buyeth corn-in the market," said another " is like a babe whose mother dies and he is given over to other nurses, but is never satisfied." Frequent also are the praises of the agricultural, as compared with the commercial, life. "He that toils after money while he has no land, what enjoyment hath he from his work?" Characteristic also is the rabbinical joy in the day of rain, which is "greater than the day on which the dead are quickened. The latter is for the righteous and wicked alike: the former for the righteous alone." "It is greater," says another teacher, "than the day on which the Torah (Law of Moses) was given. The giving of the Torah was a joy to Israel only; but rain is a joy for all mankind, and a blessing which absorbs all others." Every page of the Prayer Book marks the permanence of this sentiment in the Jewish soul.

When they were driven from their own land, the Jews of the West continued to be largely devoted to agriculture. It is not before the fourth or the fifth century that they are distinguished in commerce, or prominent for their wealth in money. In Carthage, in Spain, and in Southern France they held to their ancestral vocation, till the Church, barbarous itself after its victory over the barbarians, set itself to tear them from the soil and forced them into uncongenial callings. And the love of Nature and the desire to till the soil, though it has been but a dream for scores of generations, has never died away, any more than the yearning to return to the old home.

It is not surprising, therefore, that one of the outstanding features of the Palestinian revival has been the return of the Jew in his old land to his old way of life. Scattered up and down the country are a number of Jewish agricultural villages which are commonly spoken of as the "Colonies," and contain together a population of over 12,000 souls. The word "colony" is used in the old Latin sense of a small community engaged in agriculture, and an outpost of the higher civilisation. Nor is it in Palestine only that the Jews have returned to the peasant life. Apart from some 25,000 Jewish families (representing 150,000 persons) living on the soil in Russia, there are twice as many Jewish farmers in the Argentine as in Palestine, and nearly three times as many in the United States. In Canada, too, over 5,000 have been settled in villages of the North-

Western provinces during the last twenty years, and are prospering. These growing settlements have been promoted mainly by the Jewish Colonisation Association, the body to which Baron de Hirsch, aspiring to solve the Russo-Jewish problem by emigration back to the land, bequeathed twenty years ago a fortune of some nine million pounds. One of the Hirsch foundations in America is an agricultural college at Woodbine which trains annually about 150 pupils. The Alliance Israélite controls an agricultural school in Palestine, another in Tunis, and a third in Smyrna. The foundation of the agricultural school, *Mikveh Israel*, near Jaffa, in 1870, was the first step in the systematic settlement. It was due to the enthusiasm of a Jew of the Levant who, coming to France, proclaimed in and out of season, and in the end convinced the most completely emancipated Jewry of Europe, that the Jewish problem might be solved by the return of the Jews to life on the land.

The first colony to be founded (in 1873) was the hamlet of *Moza*, about six miles west of Jerusalem, on the site of the place where the willow branches for the Temple service at the harvest festival used to be plucked. It was followed by the foundation, in 1879, of *Petach Tikvah* (the Gate of Hope), a few miles from Jaffa, and in 1882 by the establishment of *Rischon-le-Zion*, in the same district, and

Zichron-Jakob, near Carmel, farther north. The pioneers of the colonisation were young Russian and Roumanian refugees. The first Hebrew letters to the Biblical exhortation: " O house of Israel, come let us go forth ! " gave the name " BILU," by which these pioneers were known. Some hundreds planted themselves in half a dozen other settlements during the eighties, making up for lack of farming experience by their enthusiasm. Their crops were attacked by droughts and locusts, and their bodies by malaria and fever, but by the help of Baron Edmond, head of the French house of Rothschild, who took the colonists under his wing, they were enabled to withstand the inevitable trials and losses of colonisers in a neglected country. The French administration of the Baron, it is true, brought at first a brazen yoke as well as a golden car; it was often controlled by people who had inadequate sympathy with the national idea, the adventurers and tadpoles of the philanthropic world. But one great and solid gain may be accounted to this early administration: the number of settlements increased, and the roots were firmly fixed in the soil. Gradually the bad features of the new régime became visible to the Baron, and were removed. The Jewish farmers, and the Jewish villagers, were the nucleus of the national revival, when Herzl's trumpet call transformed a student's dream into a people's awakening.

JUDÆA

In the decade preceding the war the agricultural movement in Palestine was one of the chief objectives of Zionist effort : and in 1914 there were some forty settlements ranging in population from three thousand in Petach Tikvah to less than one hundred in the smaller settlements, and comprising altogether an area of near 100,000 acres and a total population of twelve thousand. One-tenth of the Jewish inhabitants of Palestine lived in these colonies or villages, and about one-thirtieth of the soil of the country was in their hands. That is still a small proportion : but seeing that only eight per cent of the whole land area of Palestine is fully cultivated, and that the Jewish settlements are everywhere oases of development amid the wilderness of half-cultivation and neglect, the colonies play a larger part in the life of the country than their size and population might suggest. They play a still more striking part in the Jewish life. They are outposts of the new Hebraism, the first rough sketches of the Jewish community which is to be; and, under the influence of the national movement, they will develop into the full picture.

PETACH TIKVAH is the largest as well as almost the oldest of the settlements, and that which the Jewish visitor usually sees first, because it lies near to Jaffa. When you have travelled along the Jaffa-Nablous road for a few miles, past the neat houses and the well-ordered fields of the German Templars' village of Sarona, there can be seen stretching away to the east the green freshness of orange orchards, the rich tilth of well-cultivated fields, and the clustering of red-tiled roofs which bespeak the meeting of the West and East. The coming and going of waggons and American carts bearing Hebrew signs, and full of men and women who derive unmistakably from the Ghetto, prepare you for the entrance to the Jewish land. You skirt a river, deep set between banks of luxurious vegetation (the Nahr-el-Auja), and you pass on to the cluster of houses amid which the synagogue and school stand out. The synagogue is a gaunt bare building. It has been compared by a non-Jewish observer to a " Methodist chapel, puritanical in its whole style, reflecting the religion of an ancient and tenacious race, which has long since discarded ritual for legal codes of morality in its religious life." The writer can hardly have assisted at a service in the synagogue, or he would have found abundant survivals of ritual. But from the outside there is certainly little of the decorative, and scant appeal to the senses. The village is rather closely packed, for there was a tendency in the earlier settlements to create new Ghettoes for old. The emigrants from Russia and Roumania had been so used to live in cramped circumstances that they could not at first take advantage of Nature's spaciousness in their new home. The houses here lie close together in one or two streets, not indeed huddled pell-mell like the huts of an Arab hamlet (which are only second to Egyptian villages in unfitness for human habitation), but lacking garden space or open places. There is nothing like a village green or a common, such as gives a bright and free appearance to the humblest homes of rural England; no village pond for the ducks and geese; no cricket-pitch for the boys. It is a village community whose tie is rather in learning and literature and language, than in long association upon a particular piece of land.

In this respect the neighbouring German settlements founded by the sect of Templars, who emigrated in the "sixties" to the Holy Land to establish the good life communistically, are a better model. The homesteads have pretty gardens, and the roads are turned to avenues with shady trees. But Petach Tikvah is also now expanding on the better lines, and a good many detached villas with gardens around them have been built of late. Attached to the Colony also are two settlements of Jewish working men, "Poalim" as they are called, who are employed by the farmers and have little garden plots of their own. The chief cultivation is of oranges. The groves which cover the dunes and plains for miles around Jaffa produce the large oranges for which Jaffa is famous, and the Jewish settlers have been quick to take to a form of agriculture which gives scope to intelligence. The groves are irrigated from the river, or from artesian wells, by petrol engines, which are tended by the Jewish workmen.

It was made a reproach against the first development of Jewish colonisation that the settlers were supervisors rather than true farmers, and employed Arab labour for the work of the fields. There was a danger of landlord-colonies cultivated by the less intelligent labouring class who looked with jealous eyes on their physically inferior masters. But during the last decade the need for encouraging the employment of Jewish labour has been universally recognised. For all kinds of skilled labour the emigrant Jew of Eastern Europe is better suited than the native Arab, and a large Jewish unskilled labour force has been found in the immigrants from Arabia, who are moving rapidly into the Holy Land. The Jews of the Yemen have been largely hewers of wood and drawers of water to the Arabs, and the opening of Palestine to immigration has seemed to them a veritable beginning of the Messianic age. They have a lower standard of living than the immigrants from Europe, and a greater aptitude for bodily toil; and they have also a simple faith and a religious devotion which protects them from the restlessness of mind and body that attacks the wanderers from the European Ghetto. They live to some extent their own lives, having their own habitations and synagogues and rabbis; but their relations with the Russian Jews are perfectly friendly, and the School, the great conciliator, rapidly breaks down, in the younger generation, the line of cleavage. Education will doubtless have the effect of raising the standard of living, which may affect the fitness of the Yemenites for the field work which they do to-day; but when that change takes place a generation, it is hoped, will have grown up in the Colonies which will have more genuinely than its parents the peasant mind, and will till and plough, not as a strange occupation endured from love of the Holy Land, but as its natural work, inspired by love of the soil.

Journeying once to Palestine I met aboard the steamer a bright young boy from Petach Tikvah, the son of a teacher in the school, who had been to Europe to have his eyes treated, and was travelling with a party of Chaluka Jews of the class that spend all their time in prayer and study. When I asked him what he wanted to be when he grew up, he said he was undecided whether he wanted to be a gardener or a lawyer. The doubt was characteristic of a village boy sprung from a line of rabbis and scholars; but it was something that he should consider horticulture as a serious rival to the law for a vocation. A child of the European Ghetto would not have had regard to that possibility.

The population in the Colonies falls into two religious sections, the nationalists and the orthodox; or those who attend the synagogues and those who refrain. Many of the early colonists were drawn from the pious communities in Jerusalem and so-called Holy towns, and had previously spent the better part of their days in prayer and study. They represent the extreme standpoint of religious observance which has been intensified by the life of the Ghetto. Some of the more recent settlers and the Poalim or working men, on the other hand, are drawn from the emancipated youth of Russian Jewry, to whom the Haskala, or "Enlightenment," movement has brought a revolution of ideas without any new faith or firm basis of religious belief. Non-observance is for them a principle, and they represent an extreme nationalising standpoint which has been intensified by the environment of the Ghetto. They regard Palestine as the land of free life, unhampered either by the law of the Pale or by the laws of the Bible. Religious conditions in modern Palestine started from two extremes; but in the colonies generally a middle way is being gradually reached, both for religious observance and religious teaching.

The main body in the villages holds in practice to a conservative standpoint in Judaism which is free from the rigour of the very orthodox as well as from the studied laxness of the radicals. Religious ceremonies which may seem obsolete and irksome elsewhere become natural and welcome in the villages of Judæa and Galilee. The remark of a Russian orator at one of the Zionist Congresses that in the Diaspora the Jew who seeks to be orthodox cannot avoid breaking the law, while in Palestine the Jew who is indifferent cannot avoid observance, has a measure of truth. The Palestinian Colonies are in this respect remarkably contrasted with Jewish agricultural settlements in other countries. In the Argentine and Brazil, in the United States and Canada, in the colonies which have been promoted by the Jewish Colonisation Association, Judaism seems rapidly to decay and wither away. Material prosperity brings with it materialism of thought. Though the environment is Jewish, and there is not the destructive influence of a powerful industrial civilisation, yet the religious and spiritual life are none the less rapidly submerged. On the other hand, in Palestine a conscious spiritual and religious development makes for the blending of the ideas of to-day with the national heritage. At the moment the spiritual development, showing itself in language and literature and education, is the more prominent; but by the side of the revived Hebraism, a revived Judaism is springing up which is destined to be the basis of a fresh inspiration to the Jews of the whole world.

It is on the Sabbath day that the religious

life of the Palestine settlements is best discerned. Not that the day is marked by any ceremonies unknown to the Ghetto, but a new spirit inspires the old practices. The cessation from all work throughout the village—and the Arab labourers no less than the colonists take their rest on the Sabbath—the special preparations in each household to secure the brightness of the day, the Sabbath clothes which are donned by man, woman, and child, and above all the joyousness and gaiety which characterise the village from the Friday eve to the Sabbath night—these things proclaim the realisation of the spirit of the day in a way which cannot be attained either in a European Ghetto or any Western town. The younger men, or what is equally important, the younger women, seldom indeed take part in public worship, and the synagogue remains out of touch, even to the method of pronouncing Hebrew, with the new life; but everybody is at rest, and everybody is becomingly dressed in honour of the day; the youths and maidens take their walks together; the older people pay visits to each others' homes; the reading-room and club-room—the Beth-Am (or House of the People), as it is called—is full of boys and girls speaking Hebrew to one another, or reading Hebrew journals and reviews. Here are the seeds of a Sabbath which may well be called a day of delight; not a Puritan Sabbath indeed—that was never the Jewish mode—but a day of repose with a touch of holiness, and a day on which every person may call his soul his own.

On the working days it is in the early morning and the early evening that the Jewish Colony everywhere is seen at its best. In the first hours of sunlight the colonist rides or drives out with his working tools or implements; the Arab labourer or Jewish workman leads the beasts from their stalls, the women feed their poultry, and the children troop to school. And at the setting of the sun, the men come in from their work and everybody is about in the streets, the animals are driven to their stalls, and the young people promenade. In the interval between sunrise and sunset the village itself is quiet save when the diligence starts out or returns from the larger towns, where all the marketing is done. There are few shops in the colonies. In the smaller settlements the druggist is often the one and only shopkeeper, and his is rather a profession than a trade—a busy one indeed as the colonists are keen on the wares of the apothecary. A few general dealers have established themselves in the bigger villages; but the Jewish farmers and labourers have more mobility than the ordinary countrymen, and regularly go to the town when they want to buy things.

One of the most serious problems of the colonisation movement is how to extend the area of the colonies so as to provide scope for

66 THE AGRICULTURAL COLONIES

the younger generation when they grow up and need land of their own. The Jewish immigrant has driven up the price of land : for the Arab, though backward in other things, has been awake in his appreciation of the enhanced demand. Hence, hitherto the size of the colonies has increased slowly, and the more usual method of expansion has been to acquire a tract in another part of the country and settle the young men there. A constellation of settlements is congregated around Jaffa. Besides Petach Tikvah, and its two little dependencies there are two larger settlements, *Rischon-le-Zion* and *Rechoboth*, and three smaller, *Wadi-el-Chanin*, *Katra* and *Ekron*. They all owe their origin to the enthusiasm of the Russian " Lovers of Zion." They all, except Rechoboth, which was established and has been maintained on lines of self-dependence, received a considerable measure of support from Baron Edmond de Rothschild. To-day all are free from the direct administration of the Jewish Colonisation Association (Baron de Hirsch's foundation for Jewish settlements), to which the control of the Rothschild colonies was in 1899 transferred. Most of the colonists are independent, and the rest are gradually repaying their loans to the I.C.A., as the Association is familiarly called. Their chief cultivation is of grapes and oranges, and the co-operative principle is widely established. The whole wine industry is controlled by a single co-operative society, the Société Vignéronne Co-opérative, or *Carmel*, which has its centre and its "caves," or wine vaults, at Rischon. The Baron endowed that colony munificently with a splendid wine-plant, and the vaults are said to be the third largest in the world. The wines are exported, largely to Egypt, and also to Russia, France, England and the United States, and find a good market not only among Jews, who doubtless prefer them for sentimental reasons, but also among the general public.

RISCHON-LE-ZION (First in Zion) is in many ways the favourite child of the Baron, and its red-roofed houses, peeping out amid the big trees which have grown up around it, give a striking air of prosperity. It has too, a fine park filled with tropical plants—another token of the Baron's munificence—which was designed to be a training nursery for the Judæan Colonies, and is now a pleasure-place. But Rischon has not yet altogether recovered from the enervating atmosphere of philanthropy.

RECHOBOTH is a more progressive settlement. Its name means "enlargement," and it has in fact grown within the last ten years from a few scattered houses to a colony of nearly a thousand souls. Several leaders of the Russo-Jewish culture have taken up their abode here; and the intellectual life of the place is very vigorous. I was present some years ago at a general meeting of the inhabitants, which decided on the creation of a club-house; and one could not help being struck with the public spirit which prevailed and with the power of the leader of the colony, a strong man of few words, over a gathering full of talents. The equality of men and women in the direction of communal affairs was signally illustrated by the woman's equal right of voting and speaking, and the exercise of those rights. The colonies are almost unconsciously fashioning a new relation of man and woman in the East. Equality is secured without any of the struggles which mark the process in the West: because here there is no vested interest to crush, and no unthinking mass to arouse to consciousness. Sex-equality appears axiomatic to the Jewish "intelligenzia" of Russia: it can be, and is, immediately realised in the Yishub.

The government of the Jewish village communities offers a striking example both of the growth of representative institutions, and of the effective sanction of public opinion in an intelligent people. It was the one redeeming point of the Turkish régime that, not only did it not govern, but it made little attempt to govern, so that the settlements were left to develop along their own lines. There was no grant of municipal or village autonomy; but in fact autonomy existed. Almost the only work of the Turkish authorities was the collection of taxes, and this was done, not individually, but by villages. This condition of things, therefore, necessitated the appointment of a representative, or agent, among the colonists, who was the intermediary between the principal governor, the Vali, or Kaimakam, and the inhabitants of the village. The value of the harvest of the whole community was estimated, and the *U-sher* (the government tithe) was fixed on the whole: it was for the agent, known as the Mukhtar, to render this sum to the Governor, together—it is needless to say, with the usual concomitant of backsheesh for the various officials concerned. Turkish tribunals of justice, so called, existed in each district; but they were avoided for all civil affairs, and in criminal affairs were so notoriously corrupt, that an aggrieved person seldom had recourse to them. Many of the Jewish settlers retained their foreign nationality of origin, in order to escape this unsatisfactory jurisdiction.

With regard to policing the roads and hills, making highways and developing communications, guarding against disease and infection, and generally promoting the welfare of the people and the prosperity of the country, the Turkish government pursued a thorough policy of *laissez faire*, save only that it put certain obstacles in the way, by obstructing immigration, prohibiting foreign subjects from holding land, and refusing to allow buildings to be erected or extended on open lands without first obtaining a special *Kushan*, or land certificate. All these obstacles seemed designed rather as opportunities for replacing government pay of officials by private contributions, and the whole system was one of obstruction, tempered by douceurs. The Young Turks during their seven troubled years of power, before the war, had made some half-hearted and somewhat ineffectual attempts to improve things; and in Palestine they had instituted something in the way of police, which had sporadic fits of energy. They had done something, too, in the way of road-making, mainly for military purposes. But scarcely any change had taken place in the relation of the government to the Jewish village communities.

Each colony has a Committee (*Va-ad*) elected by popular suffrage, which exercises the general conduct and management of all matters of common concern. But beyond that there is no universality of system. In some cases only land-holders may have the final vote: in others a wider franchise has been conceded, and all adults living in the colony for a certain period are entitled to take part in the election of the Committee. In some cases the Committee appoints a single executive official, who is, as it were, the Mayor, and wields a large power; in others, the Committee as a whole, or a delegation of it, exercise the executive as well as the deliberative functions. The chief matters for which the local government is responsible are justice, police, schools, roads, water supply and sanitation, including medical attendance.

Justice is administered, in matters of religious law, by the Rabbi; in matters of private or civil differences, by arbitrators appointed by the Committee. So high is the repute of the Jewish justice, that the Arabs of the neighbourhood often bring before it their quarrels for settlement. The protection of the villages and fields, both against robbers or marauders and any internal trouble, is secured by the *Shomerim* (literally, Watchmen), who are the local police. They are young men, mostly Russians, who are organised for the whole of the settlements in a regular trade union, appoint their own officers, have their own rate of wages and hours of work, and are regarded with something of hero-worship. In many parts of the country they do really carry their lives in their hands, for they are liable to meet with lawless Bedouin tribes who when excited will stop at no violence. The Shomerim themselves look like Arabs of the country, dressed in flowing burnouse with their kefiyehs, or white shawls, on their heads and carbines slung over their shoulders. But they take pride in speaking Hebrew.

The water supply and the schools and medical attendance are already developed throughout the new Jewish life in Palestine on a communal basis. They are matters neither of charity, as in the old Jewish settlements, nor of private enterprise—as they are still in many European societies—but of public concern and public interest. The community levies a rate directly for these services, and also imposes a light tax for the same purpose on the sale of meat killed ritually. Failure to pay, except for good reason, is met by cutting off the supply. Moreover the control of these services by the representatives of the community facilitates the execution of any decision of the Committee (VA-AD) whether given in an arbitration or legal suit or at a public meeting. The defaulter or resister finds his water supply cut off, his children excluded from the school, his household deprived of medical help; for there is no private school or private doctor to whom to turn. The action in practice is as effective as that of the public force of the State in more regularly constituted communities, and it is sufficient, with the moral force of the Committee, to secure complete respect for the ruling of the people's representatives.

Another function of the Committee is to assess the Government tax in conjunction with the Mukhtar, equitably between the colonists. It knows the circumstances of each landowner, and so far there has been no outburst of graft or suspicion of corruption. One further development which has been mooted, and partially put in practice (in the Jaffa Suburb,

Tel-Aviv), is the taxation of improved land values so as to secure for the community the benefit which the improvement has brought. The betterment tax is in keeping with the socialistic character of the Biblical law of the Release, and its introduction shows the general line of tendency in the new settlements.

Apart from the organisation of the *Shomerim*, little has been done, as yet, to federate the village committees under provincial government, or to form any kind of central Jewish council. On one or two occasions the villages have combined together for a common purpose, such as roadmaking and sanitation, but the larger development is for the future. So far there has been a natural and spontaneous movement towards wide self-government in the most advanced form by the villages. Outward conditions have strangely favoured it, and fostered the transformation of a people who had lived for generations in the Ghetto without any free political institutions, except such as were gathered round the synagogue, into self-reliant democratic communities. That is a development of excellent augury for the future when Palestine will be a Jewish country and these village communities will form the basis of free national councils and municipalities.

Of the smaller colonies near Jaffa, WADI-EL CHANIN, KATRA and EKRON, the second offers the greatest interest and may be taken as typical. It lies hard by the probable site of the ancient Jabneh, where Jochanan-ben-Zakkai was allowed by Titus to set up the "Scholars' Garden" which saved Judaism when the Temple was destroyed. The association of the place invites to a combination of study and the cultivation of the soil; and the present settlement has achieved that combination. The village might well be called the "New Vineyard of Jabneh." The colonists are Russian Jews who came in their youth fresh from a Yeshiba to the Yishub—from the college to the colony—in order to realise the prophet's ideal. They have never lost their love of learning amid their other occupations, and they may be compared in character with the Pilgrim Fathers of New England.

A personal reminiscence of mine is suggestive of the outlook and way of living of these scholar-farmers. My first visit to Katra was on a khamsin day, the wind was blowing sand, and we were weary with our ride. I looked for a house where we might rest and accosted an old man who was sawing wood on his balcony. He came out at once and led us into the house, and showered Eastern hospitality upon us. We were a party of five and without asking a question he gave us water to wash hands and feet, couches to lie on, provisions to eat, his finest buttermilk, his best cognac to drink. He was grieved that he had no wine and that his place was ill-provided because it was near Passover. All this time he was not even sure that we were Jews, but he genuinely loved the stranger within his gates. When he found that we were Jews from England he was delighted, and when he heard that I was the son of the jurist who drew up the statutes of the Jewish National Bank (the financial instrument of Zionism) he almost jumped with joy. He brought out all his treasures, his books, his writings, his letters, his pictures, and told us his history. He had been just a *Yeshiba Bochur* (a student in a Talmudic college) and then a *Melammed* (teacher) in Russia for some twenty years. Not content with thinking Zionism, and desiring a larger life, he came to Palestine with a few enthusiasts like himself. They bought each their little plot at Katra. He had lived in the colony, its leader and counsellor for nearly thirty years, farmer-rabbi and priest in one. He was almost seventy years old now, but hale and strong and without the suspicion of a stoop, altogether a fine type of the Jew regenerated, returning to the old life of the rabbi in the national epoch, working at once with hand and mind, combining in a full sense *Derech Eretz* (The Way of the Land) with *Talmud Torah* (the Study of the Law). His tolerance and liberality were as charming as his hospitality. Fervent and proved Zionist as he was, he yet appreciated the ideal underlying Zangwill's project for the foundation of a Jewish territory elsewhere—it was the day when there was talk of an Itoland—and even respected the attitude of anti-Zionists, provided they remained Jews. Israel, he said, has been and was to be *Kahal-Amim* (a congregation of peoples), and there was no single way of righteousness for them either in religious or political life. He had lately suffered a little experience typical of the hard struggle that the pioneers on the land must face. His son caught a Bedouin thieving at night, and struck him. A few days later he was, in revenge, set upon by Arabs and, using a revolver to defend himself, shot a man dead. The hue and cry was raised and the colony was attacked. The son had to leave the country for the Jewish agricultural colony near Smyrna, and the father had to pay 1,200 francs—a large part of his savings—as blood money to the Arabs. Even so, his house was raided, and it still bore signs of the devastation, but his eyes filled with fire as he told us how he and his other son had driven off the invaders. His mother and wife were buried in the garden, each under a tree of which the fruit was dedicated to the poor. Having recounted his history he showed us the colony. Starting with his own plantation, which comprised a little vineyard, an almond orchard, maize and bean fields, he took us round the mile of planted hills and cultivated tilth which was owned and worked by the twenty colonists and their families. He pointed out with pride their distillery—the gift of Baron Edmond—and their artesian well—the gift of Baroness de Hirsch—and their school and synagogue and their chemist's shop. Every colonist had his own little library where he studied of an evening when he returned from his farming.

The new Judæa will be achieved when colonies like Katra are a hundred times multiplied and linked together in one continuous area, stretching to the River of Egypt—the Wadi - el - Arish—which was the appointed boundary of Israel's heritage. The most southerly colony to-day is *Kastinie*, the village in the plain of the Philistines, west of Ashdod. But before the outbreak of war tracts of land had been acquired further south for settlement at Djemana, east of Gaza, and around Rafa on the Egyptian side of the old frontier, where the just and firm administration of England attracted some Jewish pioneers from Russia. The war has hindered the development of this new area of Jewish enterprise, but it has revealed the wealth of the land regarded for generations as a wilderness. Once science and industry are applied to it, when the water that has for more than a year been led by pipe lines and used to maintain great armies on the land is turned on to the land itself, then indeed the wilderness of the Negeb will blossom as the valley of Sharon.

CHAPTER IV

THE COLONIES

II. SAMARIA AND THE NORTH

As in the days of the Kingdom the people were divided into two states, Judah and Israel, so in the Return the pioneers are divided into two groups—those of Judæa and those of the North. They are not, it is true, any more contending, or even rival peoples, but they have their local pretensions and their separate prides. Those of Judæa will speak of Tel-Aviv, the Jewish garden suburb of Jaffa, as the people of London will speak of the Hampstead " Garden City." Those of Galilee will point with pride, as does Sydney to its harbour, to the cluster of colonies around " Our Lake," or to the Jewish domain close to Haifa from which arises the new Polytechnic. And if, for the present, Judæa has the predominance in population because of the thousands that live in Jaffa and Jerusalem, the North has the predominance in holding of the land.

The peaceful penetration has hardly reached as yet the interior hill country of Samaria, where the mountains are separated by rolling

SAMARIA AND THE NORTH

and fertile valleys. Nablous, the ancient Shechem and the dwelling-place of the patriarch Jacob, is the home of the remnant of the Samaritan Jews who have maintained their holy place at Mount Gerizim for 2,500 years and still ascend its slopes each Passover to offer the sacrifice of the lamb; but the Jew of the West has not established himself there. Haifa, however, which is the commercial centre of all northern Palestine, as Jaffa is of southern Palestine, has become one of the chief places of the Yishub, and along the coast of the Great Sea and the shore of the Lesser Sea (of Galilee) the Jewish estate is yearly spreading.

Travelling northwards from Jaffa we reach, after a too long interval, the cluster of Jewish agricultural colonies which is known as the Samarian group. It comprises *Chederah*, *Zichron Jacob* and its dependencies (*Um-ed-Djemal* and *Schweiye*), *Athlit* and the recent settlement *Kerkur*. They all lie near the sea; Chederah, Kerkur and Athlit on the coastal plain, the others on the hills which form part of the Carmel ridge. The associations of the country link it with the Hellenistic era and the Crusaders' invasion, for along this strand were the flourishing ports of Cæsarea and Dor and Sycaminon, once brilliant with all the outward show of Greek temples, amphitheatres and colonnades. A thousand years later the mountain road was dotted with the castles of the crusading lords, of which the memory is preserved by the beetling ruins of Athlit. The most splendid of Hebrew associations with the district is the denunciation of idolatry and the declaration of God's Unity by Elijah to the children of Israel on Mount Carmel. The traditional site of that event is indeed outside the boundaries of the Jewish settlement, on the south-eastern spurs of Mount Carmel at a spot known as the *Meharika* (the place of turning), which, like many of the Biblical sites, is now marked by the presence of a monastery. But the whole ridge of Carmel is endeared as the type of what is pure and fresh and beautiful, and throughout the year that ridge is ever a delight to the eye and a spur to the imagination.

ZICHRON JACOB, the largest village of the group, with a population of nearly one thousand souls, is peculiarly happy in its setting. Standing on a hill which rises precipitously about 500 feet from the maritime plain, it surveys the whole plain of Sharon to the south, the Carmel ridge to the Bay of Acre on the north, and the hill country of Samaria, beautifully intersected with vale and slope, to the east. The road by which it is entered from the north passes through a narrow defile between two encircling arms of the hills that here make their last inroad on to the fertile plain, and render it, as it were, a preserve from the half-cultivated plain about it, which is owned or worked by Arab farmers. The Arabs can only plough, and have shown no capacity for the introduction of western methods for plantations, or scientific agriculture. The zone of each colony is clearly defined by the indication of a proper road, distinct from the rutty track which leads through the Arab villages, by the screens of trees, the hedgerows of mimosa and the better ordering of the fields. One cannot enter any colony without a thrill of feeling that here, indeed, is Jewish land, the work of Jewish hands; nor can one leave it without a pang of regret that the area thus reclaimed is still so small, and the area to be won still so large. The first colonists at Zichron planted vineyards and the fall in the world's demand for wine, coupled with an epidemic of phylloxera, having brought ruin to several, caused them to abandon their homesteads. But their place has been taken up by new settlers, and it is urgent to provide new means for the healthy expansion of the settlements.

CHEDERAH is a more spacious colony than Zichron. The holding of each colonist is large, for the land here was purchased more cheaply, being marshy, and when the pioneers first settled thirty years ago, it was infested with the malaria-carrying mosquito. Before the war the colony had been almost purged of the pest by the planting of large woods of eucalyptus, which gives it the appearance of a forest settlement. The houses are not massed together, as in the other colonies, but are separated by plantations and avenues. The afforestation serves also to check the growth of another obstacle to agriculture, the sand dunes, which threaten to encroach on the fertile plain. As our army learnt all too well, the dunes stretch already from El-Arish to Jaffa in almost unbroken array, and are making their way northwards. The sand is said to come from the Nile, and this Egyptian invasion has gone on relentlessly, year by year, unchecked by the Turks, so that miles of the most productive part of the coast have been lost. A serious effort is made in the Jewish colonies to-day to check the danger of sand-choking; and large schemes of afforestation with pines, such as the French have carried out in Tunis successfully, might altogether stop it. But the work of this planting will have to begin anew at the end of the war, for the Turks have cut down all the trees for their military requirements, and the beauty of Chederah has been felled to the ground.

From Chederah one proceeds by the road to ATHLIT, the other colony of the group. It lies by the sea-shore, and we pass on the way the scattered ruins of the Hellenistic port of CÆSAREA, and the site of the Hellenistic Doris, now covered by the Arab village of Tantura. Cæsarea was one of the proud erections of Herod, and was designed at once to manifest his

SAMARIA AND THE NORTH

loyalty to his Roman patrons and his own magnificence. Marble was brought from Alexandria for its palaces and colonnades, and by a curious irony of fate, that marble has been transported back in recent years from its ruins to Alexandria for the construction of private mansions at the Egyptian port. In the early centuries of the Christian era, Cæsarea became the chief city of the Holy Land, and was famous for its schools of learning. In the middle ages it was a famous fortress; to-day its port is represented by a ruined mole, its commerce by a few sailing barges, and its colonnades and amphitheatres by a few heaps of stones and earthworks. Some Bosnian Moslems, who were settled there by the Turks in the middle of the nineteenth century, made a sad havoc of the ruins which, till their arrival, had been imposing. The only sign of the former greatness of the place is a part of the mediæval wall on which the rude huts of the present inhabitants are now built.

TANTURA is another derelict port some seven or eight miles to the north. Here an attempt to start a glass factory, which was made by one of Baron Edmond's administrators at a most extravagant outlay, ended in failure. The record of that failure is to be seen in a tall gaunt building surrounded by palms set in a hedge of cactus. Malaria and inefficient organisation made the experiment abortive. In the middle ages, the Jews were famous craftsmen in glass, and Benjamin of Tudela, the famous traveller, who visited the Jewish communities of three continents in the eleventh century, records that small communities in Palestine were then engaged in the industry.

A few miles north of Tantura stands a narrow promontory surrounded by the Crusaders' Castle of Athlit, and hard by lies the little colony of the same name and another Jewish enterprise, more successful than the glass factory, the Jewish Agricultural Experimental Station. The colony which consists of some dozen homesteads was founded by the I.C.A. and is conducted on the *metayer* system, the tenant farmers giving a portion of their yearly produce as rent to the Association. One of the peculiarities of the Palestine colonisation came to my knowledge in this little settlement. Talking with a young farmer's wife I learnt that she was a proselyte to Judaism, a *Giyurith*. She was a Russian peasant woman and, like several others, had come out to Palestine with her husband and brought to her new home an experience of peasant life, which is rare among pure Jewesses. At Chederah likewise a few Russian " Seventh Day Baptists " are settled among the Jewish colonists, and they regard it as a matter of immense pride if one of their family is united to a Jew or Jewess. A revival of Jewish proselytism may occur in the Yishub, for it is

SAMARIA AND THE NORTH 85

not principle, but proscription, which for centuries has repressed the Jewish Mission among the Gentiles. With the return to free conditions Judaism may show its old power of expansion.

The chief present interest of Athlit is the Agricultural Station, which lies in the plain close under the ledge of Carmel. Its boundaries are unmistakably marked by the beginning and end of a piece of well-engineered roadway, which would do credit to any countryside, and is almost unique in the Holy Land. The Station is due to the energy and enthusiasm of Aaron Aaronson, the son of a Roumanian colonist of Zichron, who, having served his apprenticeship in agricultural investigation with the I.C.A. and the Turkish Government, sprang into scientific fame by the discovery of wild wheat on the spurs of Mount Hermon. He was unmoved by the offers of a professorial chair from several American universities and resolved to devote himself to Palestinian agriculture. Convinced, himself, that here was virgin scientific ground and fruitful physical soil, he knew how to convince the enlightened leaders of Jewry in the United States of the value of his idea. Julius Rosenwald, the multi-millionaire of Chicago, became president of an Association registered as an American company for the establishment of an experimental station in Palestine, and among others who were closely asssociated with the movement were Jacob Schiff and Nathan Strauss. The scheme had grown under his hand during the five years of its history before the war and the station comprised the stretch of land at Athlit, a nursery at Chederah and a chemical research laboratory and museum or library at Zichron Jacob. The fields at Athlit were a model of what all Palestinian fields might be if capital and enthusiasm were combined with science to develop them. Cleared of all stones and scientifically drained, they produce crops of monster grain which would rouse the envy of an American land-booster. They are flanked by an avenue of various trees which exemplify the varied possibilities of Palestinian horticulture. The beginnings are clearly visible of a park containing the flora of all countries which enjoy similar climatic conditions to those of Palestine. So far the Station has produced a display of the possibilities of cultivation on the land; but the more solid usefulness to which it is destined is the determination of the various species which will flourish, and the dissemination of good stocks and seeds among the colonists, and the spreading among them of the knowledge of how to train such stocks and seeds.

In GALILEE a third cluster of Jewish colonies has been planted which is quite different in character from both the Judæan and Samarian groups of settlements. The Galilean cluster falls indeed into two divisions, the one grouped around the Lake of Tiberias, the other lying on the uplands in the northern part of the country. The rabbis lovingly dwell on the variety of nature in the Holy Land, which contained, they said, twelve different provinces according to the number of the twelve tribes, each of which is a land with its different fruits and trees. George Adam Smith in our day has pointed out the extraordinary variety of the vegetation and physical conditions which are to be met with in the different sections of the country. The dividing line is the Vale of Esdraelon, or Jezreel, which separates Galilee from Samaria. South of that the general nature is sub-tropical, north of it we are in a temperate land, save in the Jordan Valley, where the vegetation and climate are similar to those of the southern part. On the hills and uplands, however, of Galilee, cornfields, olives and almonds take the place of the orange groves and vineyards of the south. The Jewish settlements are rougher and less prettily laid out than those in Judæa; at the same time more of the work is done by Jewish labour. For their foundations—with the single exception of *Rosh Pinah*—owe less to the bountiful philanthropy of Baron Edmond and are more often the creation of popular societies which have as part of their programme the encouragement of a Jewish peasant class. Two of the colonies which lie on the outskirts of Galilee, *Merchavya* in the plain of Esdraelon and

Kinnereth which nestles on the southern shores of the Sea of Galilee, were promoted by the Jewish National Fund. It is a happy feature of these colonies that they bring together the old and the new Jewish inhabitants of Palestine. In each of them may be found among the workers some who come from the more ancient Jewish agricultural settlements in the land, founded by the Turco-Jewish worthy, Joseph of Naxos, in the seventeenth century, and there are a considerable number of local Sephardic Jews. The main element of these colonies, however, consists of young Russian and Galician Jews who immigrated in the first place as labourers and were instructed in agricultural work, and are now encouraged and assisted to become the proprietors of small holdings.

At MERCHAVYA an experiment is being tried in co-operative colonisation. The settlers work under a single direction and share the profit on the year's working. Though not immediately successful in the material way the Colony, which was planted in 1911, has already made great strides in the development of the land. I spent an evening or two there in its first beginnings when the habitations were little Arab huts, with a shanty or two for the women. Malaria threatened all the settlers. A young Russian woman doctor was looking after them as fever patients; and, after our simple supper of vegetable soup and coffee, there was a quinine pill for everybody except our anti-quininists. The director of the settlement was troubled because of a threatened Arab attack. The land had been obtained from a rich Syrian-Greek landowner who dispossessed his Arab tenants to make room for the Jewish settlers. Not unnaturally those who had been turned away did not welcome their successors. Acting on the maxim of *obsta principiis*, they concocted some charge of child murder against the colonists and demanded revenge. The charge was in the end exploded, the Arabs appeased, the huts replaced by healthy and sanitary farm buildings, and the malaria largely exterminated by drainage and quinine treatment. Before the war Merchavya was smiling and the Arabs and Jews worked peaceably together. The harsh circumstances of the last three years have prevented a fair test of the economic soundness of the co-operative experiments; but the Labour party, if it may be so called, in the Zionist body will certainly press for the extension of settlements of the kind. Herzl foresaw that the Jewish colonisation would harbour all manner of ideas of the most advanced society. It is not for nothing that the Jew in Europe takes a leading part in economic and social movements. He carries with him wherever he goes—and back to his old country—the progressive mind; and his tradition moulds him to socialistic institutions. The Sabbatical year and the Jubilee of Mosaic legislation are translated in modern life into the communistic colony.

The intellectual level of many of the colonists in these labour settlements is remarkable, and even a little disquieting. It seems too high for those who are to be tied to the soil. Typical was a young Roumanian I met in Galilee, who had been educated at the Leipzig Realschule and had given up commerce for the settler's life. He was living in a simple hut, but his library comprised a Bible, a Talmud, Weber's *Welt Geschichte* in many volumes, Lessing, Goethe, Heine and Nietzsche, a complete Shakespeare in German, a number of French classics, one or two English and Hebrew novels, the modern Hebrew poets, some Zionist literature and a few dictionaries. This was not the stuff on which the peasant mind vegetates. I was not surprised to hear two years later that he had left the colony and gone to America. There is no inherent reason why the philosophical mind should not go with the peasant quality, but many of these later-day philosophers belong to the Peripatetic school, rather than to that of the Garden. It is inevitable that a considerable proportion of those who come out under the influence of a vague idealism to be pioneers should not find in the new surroundings the exaltations which they seek, and wander away. There will always be a

SAMARIA AND THE NORTH

certain wastage among the new immigrants, but the core of the population will be found in the younger generation of the settlers. If they are given the opportunity of leading " the good life " in the country, it will not matter that there is a coming and going of young men and women from the communities of the Diaspora.

It must not, however, be supposed that the immigrant from Europe is always, or even normally, an " intellectual." There is a large enough class of the pure workman type, who are ready to be moulded into farm workers in the hope of ultimately becoming farmers. In Galilee there are two training colonies for men of this kind; *Sedjera*, on the flank of Mount Tabor, between Nazareth and the Lake, and *Medjdel* by the site of the ancient Magdala on the borders of the Lake.

SEDJERA was founded by the I.C.A. with the purpose of producing a more independent type of colonist than the farmer of the Baron's colonies. All the work was to be done by the Jewish workman and the life was rigidly simple; each homestead contained a bed-room, a living room, and a kitchen. Most of the colonists were unmarried, and for a time they received a living wage from the administration till they had acquired some skill in the work of the field. Among them I met an English settler, a man who had spent some years in London, tailoring, but who found ten francs a month and board in Palestine better than thirty shillings a week in Whitechapel. The I.C.A. has since disposed of the land to the Jewish National Fund, but the functions and objects of the settlement have remained unchanged.

MEDJDEL is a Russian working-men's colony which was taken over in 1909 by a Zionist group in Moscow from the German Templars, who had not made a success of the settlement. In 1911 some hundred young Jewish men were working there under the direction of a very energetic agronomist who combined the parts of administrator, doctor, architect and secretary. Some half-dozen women were among the workers, and a disproportionate number of children. Many of the men came out with their children, and sent for their wives afterwards. To manage men in Palestine you must have some linguistic accomplishments, and the director talked Hebrew with the children, Jargon with some of the older people, and Arabic with the natives. The cultivation was partly of the regular Palestinian crops and partly of cotton. Water was abundant, the land was easily irrigated from the lake, and there was abundant heat, so that the cotton-growing experiment promised good results. Under a progressive administration the whole Jordan Valley could be turned by simple engineering work into an irrigated plain, like the Nile Valley, and not less productive.

A number of Jewish colonies already exist round the Lake of Tiberias which only require linking up to form a continuous Jewish region. From the colony of *Melchamyeh*, south of the Lake, and *Kinnereth*, which lies by the outflow of the river, the line runs along the slopes between the banks, through *Poria*, *Yemma*, *Bedjen* and *Sedjera* to the city of Tiberias, which is almost entirely Jewish in population, and then beyond it through *Medjdel* to *Yesod-Hamaaleh* and to *Rosh Pinah*, which lies on the hills to the north of the lake. Between these two last colonies and the rest there is a rather large gap in the Jewish territory, but no considerable Arab village occupies the interval. All this part of Galilee was in the early part of the Christian era famous for its fertility and its beauty. To-day the region to the east of the lake is deserted; an attempt at a Jewish colony there, the *Bnei-Yehuda*, was not successful because the right people were not chosen for the enterprise, and the marauding Bedouins frightened the new-comers away. But nature has marked out the whole region for fruitfulness; it is a vast hothouse, with an immense reservoir for the purposes of cultivation, and if human industry is well applied its former glory will be revived.

The most hopeful development in the modern colonisation has been the American plantation of PORIA, which was founded some seven years ago by the Zionists of St. Louis. It is the first of the so-called "Achuzah" schemes to be realised, and is auspicious of what may be done by American enterprise combined with Jewish idealism. The idea of the Achuzah is that a number of small capitalists in the west should combine to acquire a tract of land in Palestine for their own benefit and have it worked by Jews of the country till they are ready to come out and settle. Some may take up their inheritance at once, others simply receive their share of the fruits of the plantation. The defects of the system of absentee landlordism are avoided by the common national sentiment. Many Achuzah societies have beeh founded—among them an important one in England, the Maccabæan Land Company—but so far, besides Poria, only one such settlement has been planted. The movement for colonisation on these lines was in full swing when the war broke out and stopped all activity. But when peace is restored it will be a fine achievement for these societies to link up the Galilean colonies with a continuous line of plantations. The few American settlers who are already in the land have brought an energy and initiative which are often lacking in the colonists from Eastern Europe. It was at Melchamyeh that I met a colonist who was watering orange plants and banana trees in his garden, the only man in

SAMARIA AND THE NORTH 95

the village who possessed such delights. The colonist turned out to be a Russian Jew who had been for many years a farmer in Minneapolis, U.S.A. Falling ill there he was told that he must live in Palestine or Italy, and his wife insisted on Palestine. He was no Zionist and rather sighed for the beer and the flesh-pots of Minneapolis, but he found compensation in the excellence of the land and the climate, and declared that, with a settled government, the change of farming from the West to the East would also be a profitable enterprise.

The last group of Jewish colonies are those which lie in the northern part of Galilee. *Rosh-Pinah* ("the Corner Stone") and its satellites *Yesod-Hamaaleh* at the southern end of the Lake of Merom; *Mishmar Ha-Jarden* and *Machanaim* by the upper waters of the Jordan; and *Metullah*, a mountain village at the lower spurs of Hermon. They have all striking situations, but to-day they give the impression of having seen better days. At first vineyards were here, as in Judæa, the chief cultivation, but while the orange gardens have elsewhere provided a fresh outlet for enterprise, in these more temperate regions they could not be introduced, and corn and almonds, which are now largely grown, are not yet as profitable. Perhaps it is defective road communication, for there is no proper highway to the Lake; perhaps lack of resource in the colonists ; perhaps the malaria which in the settlements by the river did its evil work, sapping the vigour of the little community ; but certainly the spirit of hopefulness is less evident here than in the newer centres of Lower Galilee and Samaria. A fresh impulse from without is required to make the colonies of Northern Galilee as virile as those of the South.

METULLAH, the most northern outpost, is acquiring a new function as a summer resort for the rest of the country. Its mountain air and its splendid site, high up above a ravine, down which a stream dashes headlong to Jordan, makes it a chosen place in the dry days, and already its few homesteads are crowded in July and August. Metullah is a summer station for the hardy men and women of the colonies ; it lies too far from the high road to attract the tourist, but in course of time it, or some other place in the highland region, will become for the Jewish dwellers of the lowlands what a number of hill stations in the Lebanon are already to the Syrians of the plains.

The Jewish traveller who does not restrict his time to the round of the chief towns and the Jewish villages can hardly fail to be struck by the smallness of the area still worked by Jewish hands. It is almost a Pale of Settlement, under free conditions. He may ride for days over hill and vale without seeing a

Jewish farmstead or passing a Jewish waggon. From the great plain of Esdraelon through Jenin, and through Nablous and the centre of the country to Judæa, or from Jerusalem southward through Hebron to Beersheba, or again along the whole length of the country east of the Jordan, through the Hauran and Gilead and Moab, the way leads through hills that still show the lines of old terraces, and through plains strewn with the ruins of ancient villages and towns, with never a sign of a Jewish settlement. This is the wide field for future enterprise; all this area cries out for an industrious and sturdy population to develop its resources. No children of Anak inhabit them to-day.

Wandering tribes of Bedouins and sparse settlements of Arabs divide the TRANSJORDANIA region, but there is room for another two and a half tribes of Israel, who would revive its old prosperity. Half a century ago Oliphant planned his scheme for a large Jewish colonisation here, based on a Turkish charter to be backed by the European Powers. But the scheme was not followed up, and the only footing which has been attempted is the purchase by Baron Edmond de Rothschild of a considerable tract of Hauran land which, however, has remained in the possession of the Arab cultivators. An overseer of the property maintains lonely supervision. No overflow from the western villages has yet made its way east. Occasionally a Jewish pedlar plies his trade in the little towns, and a few such settle and form new communities. At Beisan, the ancient Scythopolis and the famous seat of Hellenistic culture, a Russian Jewish apothecary told me that there were four or five families like his and as many Sephardim (oriental Jews) in the place engaged in petty trade. He had a story that Beisan was to be acquired by the Zionist organisation, and be the centre of a new Jewish agricultural region. The story will come true when the crown lands of the Turkish Sultan, of which Beisan is part, come into the market. Then the Jewish agricultural domain will be something more than a fringe and a series of oases. The Jewish belt will spread out eastward and westward, and Jews will share the whole country with the Arabs in friendly emulation. Then we shall be able to speak of a Jewish country, instead of Jewish colonies. But this development will require a more wholehearted effort of the entire Jewish people than Palestinian colonisation has yet evoked.

But 60,000 of the Babylonian exiles returned with Zerubbabel to Judæa to form the nucleus of the restored Commonwealth. Before the war double that number of Jews had their home in Palestine, and were the pioneers. It is now necessary to organise on an altogether fresh scale the immigration into the country. Thirty years have seen the development from the impulsive movement of little groups of enthusiasts aided by philanthropic organisation to the systematic effort of nationalist societies to build a Jewish centre. But the effort of the whole nation to make Palestine a Jewish country and a national Home remains for the new era, which the world revolution has now ushered in. When peace comes, the time will have arrived to sound the trumpet, to raise the banner, and to gather the exiles from the four corners of the earth. Then the promise of prophecy will be in the way of fulfilment: " And the seed shall be prosperous, the vine shall give his fruit, the ground shall give her increase, and the heavens shall give their dew; and I will cause the remnant of this people to possess all these things."

CHAPTER V

JERUSALEM

A GREAT city is the type of a great idea,—ancient Athens of art; ancient Rome of empire; London of liberty; New York of enterprise. Jerusalem is the type of religion. Not only is the Holy City the centre to which three of the greatest religious communities look with peculiar veneration, but its site and its buildings are full of religious associations, and almost breathe the religious idea. Its Hebrew name is explained allegorically by the sages of old as meaning either "the abode," or "the vision" of peace: and, by a false etymology, the idea of holiness was imparted into its Greek and Roman names, Hiero-Solyma. The modern Arabic name, El Kuds, conveys more definitely the same notion of holiness. It means simply the holy place, the root being the same as the Hebrew *Kadosh*.

The religious character of Jerusalem is not only a matter of history, but is imprinted almost in every foot of the soil on which it stands, and on all its surroundings. Each step you take is literally thick with religious memories, and the records of the past sink deep below the ground. Some of the streets of the modern city are 100 feet above the level of the older ways, the average depth being from 40 to 60 feet, and between them and the ancient foundations are layers on layers of civilisation. It is difficult, indeed, to reconstruct the topography of the city as it was in the days of the Temple and the Jewish national life, because the interior valleys which once separated the hills of Zion and Moriah and Ophel that lay within the walls, have been filled up with the dust of ages.

In the 4,000 years which have passed since Abraham, fleeing from Chaldæa, met and was blessed by Melchizedek, priest of Salem, the town has been destroyed again and again and, as often, arisen afresh. It has been the centre of an age-long fight between two religions; it has suffered many earthquakes, twenty sieges and eighteen reconstructions. The Psalmist spoke of it as splendid in elevation and "the delight of all the earth," a city which is all compact together. Its nature has not changed. It still rises proudly in a kind of splendid isolation from the bare hills of Judæa upon two rocky spurs that overlook the country for miles around and are entrenched on three sides by abrupt ravines. It has the aspect of a vast sanctuary, hedged off from the common world of traffic and industry. No highway of commerce passes through it;

no river here invites communities to assemble together; no fertile plain around nourishes a teeming population. It has never had any considerable commercial importance, nor, apart from the passionate loyalty which its historic sites aroused, had it any strategic value. Before David conquered it and made it the capital of his kingdom, it was the fortress of the Jebusites, and it has remained, through all its varying fortunes, a stronghold difficult of approach. The old invaders of Palestine, whether from north or south, had regularly to conquer the rest of the country before they could lead their armies from the northern plateau against it. Even Napoleon on his triumphant march from Egypt to Acre did not dare turn aside to enter it, and General Allenby did an unparalleled thing when he captured it by an encircling movement from the south and west.

Nature has fitted Jerusalem to be a city of a special type. It lies on the watershed between the east and the west, between the desert and the sea, facing the wilderness and the sirocco, yet so close to the Mediterranean as to feel the full sweep of its rains and humid winds. It thus enjoys a temperate climate, and a rainfall equal to that of London, though almost all the rain falls in four months of the year. It is perched 2,600 feet above the level of the Western sea that glimmers in the sun thirty-four miles away; and the mountains

JERUSALEM

go sheer down on the east side to another sea —the Dead Sea—some 1,300 feet below that level. The splendours of nature lie spread out to the observer standing on the top of its hills. Here, looking eastwards, he sees the abyss of the Dead Sea, the Jordan threading its way to it through the Wilderness, the blue Mountains of Moab rising precipitous on the further side of the river and this great collection of its waters. Northwards are the terraced hills, and then the bare limestone plateau of Judæa. Westward and southward, beyond the ravines which guard the city, there is the half-wild, half-cultivated country leading down into the plain. It is impossible not to be moved by a panorama so eloquent of the Divine might and human insignificance.

At night, especially, when the guides and tourists are at rest and the rumbling carriages no longer whirl up the dust, and all that is tawdry is hidden, the old city of Jerusalem weaves an extraordinary spell and is almost overpoweringly serious and solemn. In the Rabbinical literature it is said that it was a city of Joy—nobody should be troubled or concerned with business within it ; and a Hill of Accounts was selected outside the city to which everyone who had business repaired (*Sifri* Numb. 35, 10). To-day business affairs are settled inside its walls, but amusements and entertainments seem to be almost as rigidly banned as were accounts of old. Within the walled area there is no single pleasure-hall, but only meeting-places for solemn assembly, churches, convents, monasteries, schools, synagogues. Without the walls an enterprising Greek had erected, before the war, a cinema to lure the Arab, and an occasional café flared up along the Jaffa and the Bethlehem roads. A progressive municipality, emulating European ways, had installed arc-lamps along the chief streets in the suburbs, which took away from its unworldly character; and of recent years, frequent menaces of electric-trams and motor-buses have been heard, which, however, have not taken on the ugly shapes of reality. And the railroad which has already forced its way has its station a respectful distance from the walls. The day, doubtless, will come soon when other appanages of civilisation will force their way, too, into the outer purlieus, but the inner enclosure will long resist vulgarisation, because nothing less than an earthquake or a big fire could make the invasion possible.

There are, indeed, already two Jerusalems: the city of the storied past, occupying the ancient hills of Zion and Moriah and girt around with walls and crammed with monuments and sacred sites; and the city of the relentless and restless present, spreading shapelessly away to the north, without order or plan, and teeming with philanthropic institutions and religious foundations. The old city knows but two roads through which a carriage may pass, and its ways are stone steps, often vaulted over, so that you seem to be in some subterranean chamber; but the new city is a maze of crooked streets and alleys through which the crazy carriages thread their way.

The ravines which bound the city on three sides check expansion to the east, west and south, and so it is away on Mount Scopus and along the Jaffa road, where the ridge is continuous, that the ever-growing population plants its homes. Like New York, which is framed on three sides by the sea and its two great rivers, and so has spread up the Island of Manhattan, so Jerusalem, penned in by the valleys of Kedron and Hinnom, stretches away over the northern heights. The growth of the city during the last century, and more especially during the last fifty years, has been striking. Chateaubriand, the romantic writer, who was there in 1808, a few years after Napoleon's invasion of the country, described it as a City of Desolation. " Not a creature to be seen in the streets, not a creature at the gates, except now and then a peasant, gliding through the gloom, concealing under his garments the fruits of his labour, lest he should be robbed of his hard earnings by the soldiers." When Robinson, the American archæologist, visited it in 1838, its population was 11,000, composed of 4,500 Mohammedans, 3,500 Christians, and 3,000 Jews. In 1860 there were only a few houses outside the walls, and Sir Moses Montefiore made a startling innovation when he provided land for a suburban colony of Jews about a quarter of a mile from the Jaffa gate. Twenty years later in 1880 before the great immigration from Russia began the Jewish population had risen to 15,000. After that it went on increasing by leaps and bounds, and at the outbreak of war in 1914 out of a total of 100,000 more than half, some 60,000, were Jews.

There is no large city in which the proportion of the Jewish to the total inhabitants is so great, and there is no place in the world, not even New York, with its million Jews, where the Jewish population is so representative of every section and class of Jewry. Already they have begun to stream in from the four corners of the earth, just as in the time when the Temple stood, they came up to the Metropolis of their nation. Here you find kaftanned and gaberdined Jews from every ghetto of Eastern Europe; eager-looking students from the universities of the west; tall, commanding figures clad in cloth of gold from Bokhara and Turkestan, and, living near them, poor weak immigrants from Yemen and Persia, hoping equally to hasten the day of the coming of the Messiah; dignified but indolent Sephardim from the near East, side by side with the hustling Americanised Ashkenazis, or the highly-strung Russian

Revolutionaries, half intoxicated with modern thought.

Of the many Jewish settlements or colonies, the most brilliant, outwardly, is that of the Jews of Bokhara. They are rentiers, mostly older men who, having secured material ease in their native homes, come to Jerusalem to devote themselves to study and mystic contemplation. Religiously they belong to the Chassidic and Cabbalistic section, but materially they are very differently placed from the Chassidim who come from the ghettoes of Galicia and Russia. Physically, too, they are fine figures of men; tall and upstanding, with shaven polls, clad in splendid raiment from the bazaars. They tower, like Saul, above their brethren and show what the Jew may be when he is not crushed by persecution. They are somewhat detached from the rest of Jerusalem Jewry, having their own synagogues and their own schools; but the aloofness is breaking down among the young, and it will disappear in a generation. The old Eastern communities, the Persians, the Yemenites, and the Aleppo Jews, are poor, but they earn their livelihood as skilled and unskilled labourers, carriage drivers and porters, and they depend far less on the Chalukah (the eleemosynary fund), than the Jews of the West. The Yemenites of the town are generally builders or masons; they will have their opportunity after the war when the rebuilding is undertaken. Their ideas of beauty, however, are still elementary. A deputation came to me to appeal for my aid in obtaining arc-lamps for their synagogue, which was at the time lighted by old candelabra. The Persians had recently acquired one of the new "Lux Lamps" and this excited their emulation.

No Jewish community, however remote, is unrepresented at Jerusalem. Even the Falashas of Abyssinia, a strange survival of the first exile, mixed with foreign and strange elements, who have been cut off from the catholic conscience of Jewry for 2,000 years, have sent students there to be trained in the school of a broader Judaism, and so to be fitted to bring their brethren into touch with the congregation of Israel. In New York, indeed, you may find nearly all these types, but there they are in the process of being de-Judaised or Americanised. Here they are being fused into a new Hebraic community. If New York is, as it has been described, a "melting-pot" for the Jews, Jerusalem is a refiner's hearth which purifies even the dross.

The Jewish settlements stretch away to the north and north-west, from the Damascus Gate to the Jaffa Gate. The older Jewish quarter within the walls lies to the south on the lower part of Mount Zion. It is a maze of crooked lanes, sadly congested and unrelieved by a single fine building or beautiful monument. There is, it must be admitted, something in Baedeker's comment: "The Jewish quarter offers nothing of interest, but consists of a number of dirty and malodorous streets." The Mohammedans have their gorgeous Dome of the Rock; the Christians have the Church of the Sepulchre, which if not lovely is imposing, and the Armenian Convent which is both; the Jews, who are the largest community, can boast as yet of nothing noble, or worthy of their past, in the buildings of the old city. Two large synagogues of the Ashkenazi communities stand out from the mass of meeting-places, and their domes are prominent in views of the city; but they are undistinguished save in size. One, known as the "Synagogue of the Fall of the City," associated with Rabbi Jochanan-ben-Zakkai, the saviour of Judaism after the destruction of the Temple, is, as it were, the Great Synagogue of that ritual. Here the saintly Rabbi Salant, who by force of character obtained the headship over the myriad Rabbis of his time (the latter half of the nineteenth century), used to preside and give his judgments. As a building it is garish, and the decorations, illustrating certain of the Psalms, but without any representation of the human figure, are grotesque; a collection of harps and willows represents the captives hanging their lyres upon the trees by the river of Babylon, when they refused to be comforted for the destruction of their home. Some of the Sephardic synagogues are older, but architecturally of small account. But historically several of the smaller Houses of Assembly are of deep interest.

Jerusalem offers not only the microcosm of present-day Jewry, but also an epitome of the history of Judaism. Judaism has never loved sects; only the main stream has strength to flow perennially. But the sectarians that have broken away from the catholic body have still their lingering remnants in the centre of the religion. The Karaites, maintaining their succession from the Jewish Protestants of the early Middle Ages, hold assembly in a small dark room. They will have no light kindled in their habitations on the Sabbath. Still numerous in South Russia and in Cairo they lacked a *Minyan*—the ten male adults required to form a congregation—in Jerusalem when I was there a couple of years before the war. The tenth adult had recently died and there was no one to take his place. Another small community in Jerusalem which, however, has a deeper root in Jewish feeling than the Karaites, is that of the extreme Cabbalists, who pray standing and clad in robes of white. Whenever they pronounce the name of God they indulge in a kind of intense and audible concentration which is called " Zimzum." Their outward peculiarities reflect the intense devotional character of their religion. Mysticism, the seeking for an ecstatic union with the Godhead, has been at all times since the Psalmist wrote an essential aspect of Judaism—as indeed it is of every living religious creed—and these devotees in Jerusalem are in the lineal succession from Philo and the Chassidic Rabbis who "extracted the sweetness of the mystery." They attach, as our mystics have been wont to do, especial veneration to the Song of Solomon, and they chant it every Friday eve. On the occasion when I was at their synagogue one particular zealot stayed on after the congregation had left, repeating the song in a perfect frenzy and swaying as though possessed by some spirit.

The great religious meeting-place of all the Jews of Jerusalem is the KOTEL HAMAARABI, the western Wall of the Haram or Temple area. In the Middle Ages it was known as the Wall of Mercy. To-day it is inscribed in the guide-books as the Wailing Wall. It is made of rough stones, larger than those of the Gizeh Pyramids, rising to a height of 100 feet from the base, and, according to tradition, it is a part of Solomon's Temple. It is the only portion of the Haram, or Temple area, to which the Jews have access. Along the foot of the wall runs a narrow causeway, where, without shelter and with scarce room to move, stand hundreds of the still mourning people, male and female, weeping and praying.

They group themselves in clusters of twenty to fifty, each group following its own service, and the pious pass from one cluster to another. They come at all hours of the day and every day, but especially on the Sabbath eve and the Sabbath morning. There are Jews of every type and of varied garb. Sephardim in their turbans and tarbush and their Eastern garments, Ashkenazim in their felt and plush hats and their gaberdines. On the Sabbath the Ashkenasim wear their long plush robes and their fur-trimmed hats which they bring from the Ghetto of the Middle Ages. And if you descend, just after sunset, the dark and narrow cobbled lanes, shut in by stone walls, which lead to the place, and suddenly come across parties of strange figures returning from the Wailing Wall you feel carried as it were into another world. The scene at the wall itself has a poignant sadness; it represents the exile of the spirit, which is a bitterer thing than the exile from the land. Yet this bare fragment marks in a wonderful way the unity of Judaism through time and space, and its abiding spirit. The faces of the whole community of the Diaspora are turned towards it in prayer; and it is this national monument, not the resting-place of an individual, which is the Jew's supremely holy spot. Refusing to recognise in it the symbol of ruin he makes it the corner-stone of regeneration. Christianity and Islam venerate in Jerusalem scenes hallowed by the lives of their two founders. Judaism recognises no single founder and no single prophet, but centres its thoughts and hopes about the old national life and the coming national restoration.

Zangwill has recently remarked that " the Jew at the Wailing Wall is a far more poetic figure than the Jew in Wall Street; yet neither will rebuild the Wall!" But a generation which will do that, which believes that work is the true prayer, is already settling in Jerusalem; and it awaits only a modern Cyrus,[1] and a modern Nehemiah, to give it the lead in restoring the visible sanctuary of Judaism. Characteristically its principal achievement so far has been the establishment of Hebrew schools. But this generation includes architects and painters, masons and craftsmen, as well as teachers and rabbis. They are the chief builders of the city. Ever since the destruction of the Temple of Herod by Titus the school has been the hearth of Judaism, and the rabbis (teachers), not the priests, have been the popular leaders. The Great Synagogue of the future, like the Great Synagogue of the pre-Christian epoch of which the foundation is ascribed to Ezra, will

[1] Only a few months after this was written the Proclamation of Cyrus had received its modern parallel in the Declaration of the British Government (November 2nd, 1917), pledging England's efforts to secure the re-establishment of the Jewish national Home in Palestine.

be a learned faculty rather than a priestly hierarchy.

The holy area on Mount Moriah known as the Haram-el-Sharif (the noble Precinct) is now crowned with the Dome of the Rock which is ascribed to Omar, the Arab conqueror of Jerusalem, and is popularly known as his mosque. According to the tradition of Islam Mount Moriah is miles nearer to heaven than any other spot on the earth, and thence Mohammed made his journey to the celestial sphere. The dome is built over the stone on which Isaac was bound for sacrifice. According to the tradition of Islam the stone is the centre of the earth and is suspended miraculously from the ground. In the eyes of the Moslem world the Haram is the third most holy place, ranking only after Mecca and Medina. Unlike those religious shrines it is among the world's most beautiful monuments. It covers an area of about thirty-five acres (one-sixth of the entire city within the walls) and the grassy court, the cypresses, and the flashing fountains which are set about the central dome are delightfully restful after the jostle and noise of the narrow lanes. They make the same appeal as the courts of the colleges at Oxford and Cambridge. Here it seems all men may meet in peace and recognise amid the beauty of Nature and the beauty of Man's handiwork, the glory of the common Father. In another respect this holy area is fitted to be the centre of the religious life of the world. Within its borders there is not only the Jewish Temple wall, but one of the great basilicas of early Christendom, now the Mosque of El Aksa. In the new era, though it may remain the special religious demesne of the Moslems, the Haram must be opened freely to men of all creeds.

The Jews will need go a little further afield for the site of their new rallying place. The Mount of Olives, to the east of the Temple, which was of old connected with it by a wonderful gold bridge that spanned the Vale of Kedron, is, in all but historical association, the fitting site for the central home and head quarters of the Jewish Renaissance. The view that its heights command is inspiring. In front, the whole of the city with the area of the ancient Temple in the foreground, and around, the wilderness of Judæa, the Dead Sea, the mountains of Moab and the rolling hills of Judah—the country from which Amos received his inspiration, and Jeremiah, Isaiah and Zechariah spoke their messages. A great College on this site could hardly fail to fill young men and women (and it must surely be for both) with the spirit of the Prophets, and send them forth with a fresh message to humanity.[1]

[1] The great house and lands of the late Sir John Gray Hill on the Mount of Olives has since been acquired by the Zionist Organisation as the seat of the future National University.

Thus far the Jewish population has tended to expand not to the east of the city where this new Acropolis of the Hebrews may arise, but northwards. And there is nothing so far in the outward show of their expansion to arouse pride. They are spreading over the hills much as they spread in New York over Harlem and the Bronx quarters, putting up schools and synagogues between the monotonous rows upon rows of mean dwellings, but blotting out in the process the sweet fairness of Nature. The only free space left in the midst of this wilderness of bricks is " Abraham's Vineyard," a missionary enterprise where some hundred Jews are employed in tilling the ground and planting it with olives and making soap of the berry. For the rest the new-comers have contrived to reproduce in the fair fields outside the walled city the squalor and congestion of the Ghetto within the walls. They have erected long rows of barrack-like buildings facing each other across narrow and crooked streets, so that the people see nothing but the rooms opposite to theirs and can only look sadly in each others' faces.

At Jaffa the Yishub (the return) has a fitting habitation—the garden suburb of Tel-Aviv, the Hill of Spring—as the outward expression of the new Jewish spirit of hopefulness and progress in the country. But in Jerusalem the outer life and the inner are not yet at one. Some attempt towards bettering housing conditions has been made by the Sir Moses Montefiore Testimonial Trust, which has assisted building societies to lay out decent roads with neat cottages. But the capital of the Trust is little more than £10,000, and Jerusalem is in need of a large and heroic housing reform, and the thorough cleansing of some sanitary Hercules. The hills about it should be covered by garden settlements where every householder will live under his own vine and his own fig-tree. The ground indeed could be converted without much difficulty into a park-like demesne; for there is abundance of rain water in the winter and plentiful springs in the hills around. And yet to-day the town has no regular water supply, though sixty years ago the Baroness Burdett-Coutts offered to furnish it, only to meet with invincible Turkish obstructiveness.[1]

Men only require to respond to Nature's invitation to make the outer city as beautiful as the inner city is impressive. A settlement like the "American colony," as it is called, shows what a little loving care and Western order may effect. In that communistic settlement, the outcome of the aspiration of Swedish and American mystics to achieve the good life, which is strikingly told in Selma Lagerlof's *Jerusalem*, there is a delightful

[1] The want has now been supplied by the energy of the British Army of Occupation, whose Engineers have brought a continuous supply of fresh water from the hills.

garden full of cypresses and flowering shrubs and vine and fig-trees. The estate of the late Sir John Gray Hill on the Mount of Olives, surrounded by a plantation of pines and carob trees, proves likewise that fertility is yet in the soil and is the sure reward of industry. All the limestone terraces, now half ruined but still clearly marked, and all the rocky slopes of the hills of Judæa from which the soil has been washed down, may be made again smiling and fruitful with the olive and the vine so that a belt of green may be set around the stony masses of Mount Zion.

Jewish Jerusalem is not pieced out with particular sites and venerated monuments covering such spots. The whole place and all the surroundings are dense, and crowded, with memories. Apart from the Temple wall there is, however, not one which is identified. But outside the city, by the Damascus Gate, there is a cluster of caves and tombs which are historic: the grotto of Jeremiah, whose native village of Anatoth lies but six miles away, the reputed tomb of Zachariah, the prophet of the new Jerusalem, and the so-called Tombs of the Kings. These last are not of the kings of Israel and Judah, as the name suggests, but of the royal house of Adiabine, a little state in Mesopotamia, whose rulers were converted to Judaism in the first century of the Christian era and aided the Jews in their struggle against Rome. Their sepulchres, with their traces of Hellenistic art, are the one outward sign of the spiritual empire which the Jewish people wielded before they lost their national independence. Outside the walls, on the east, the Pool of Siloam recalls the earlier struggle for national liberty. From thence Hezekiah brought by a tunnel the water supply into the city when Sennacherib was camped around with the host of Assyria, and called on him to surrender. One of the few archæological treasures of the Judæan kingdom was discovered some thirty years ago when a workman struck on the stone which commemorated the meeting of the two parties of tunnellers who were working through the rock from opposite ends. The inscription records their joy at the indication that their work was meeting with success. Legends and fairy stories have gathered around the reputed tombs of David and Solomon on Mount Zion, which are now covered by a mosque. Here from time immemorial, tradition has recorded the storing of fabulous wealth and the miraculous defeat of all attempts to touch it.

Another site outside the walls which is even less certainly genuine, but is nevertheless the object of special reverence, is the Tomb of Rachel, some five miles along the road to Hebron. A spot between Jerusalem and Bethlehem has been marked by a long tradition as the resting-place of the Patriarch's wife; thither those who pray and weep at the Wall go to pray and weep again. " Rachel weeping over her children" is the symbol of grief for the destruction of Jerusalem in Jeremiah's prophecy. The wall and the tomb are the two special monuments of the national tragedy. Not far from each is a monument of the national glory, both attributed to King Solomon, who became in Jewish legend the type not only of wisdom but of material magnificence and political power. Beneath the Temple area are stretched long subterranean caverns reputed to be Solomon's stables; and beyond Bethlehem in a basin of the Judæan hills are three large reservoirs known as the Pools of Solomon, " those superb relics of inimitable magnificence," as the author of *Tancred* calls them in his extravagant rhetoric. The pools still provide water for the Temple area by means of an underground conduit, and modern engineering will in time convert them into sources of supply for part of the city.

Christian Jerusalem is to-day a maze of institutions, jostling together in a strange medley, monasteries and convents, schools and churches, mission halls and hospitals, hydropathic institutes and orphanages. The Russians have the most imposing array. Near to the Jaffa Gate a vast pilgrims' Close houses thousands of simple peasants in the holy season; and on the Mount of Olives a big monastery, flanked by a belfry, commands the whole country and is the landmark for miles as you approach. The British Army, camped around Gaza before General Allenby's rapid advance on Jerusalem, had this distant tower as its magnet. The Russian mujiks who throng the streets about Easter are the most picturesque and devout of the Christian pilgrims. The buildings of the other Christian Powers are not less imposing, but they are so stony and so empty that they seem to have no heart. They are more like fortresses than houses. The Germans with their trained sense for imposing on the Oriental mind, erected after the visit of their Emperor William four great buildings, where they could be felt and seen by all; a massive Protestant Church within the city, a massive Roman Catholic Church near the Hebron road, a massive Roman Catholic Hospice outside the Damascus Gate and a massive Protestant Hospice on the Mount of Olives, said to have been used later as the headquarters of the Turkish Army. North, south, east and west the German eagle must make his showy flight. The Emperor, who had had a way cut through the walls previously, for his carriage to enter Jerusalem, certainly left more of a mark upon the imagination of the Arabs than any other modern European figure, but his passage is written big and ugly.

The French, as heirs of the Frankish

kingdom of the twelfth century, protectors of the Roman Catholic Church from the middle of the nineteenth century, have striven not to be outbuilt by the Germans. The English Protestants have but modest buildings compared with those of the other Powers; but a new cathedral was nearly complete when the war broke out. Among the homes of the Eastern Christian Church, the American monastery on the south side of the city is a place of beauty and restfulness because of the trees in its garden. The Abyssinian Copts have their cathedral in the midst of the new Jewish quarter. Every Christian sect, indeed, has its priestly embassy at the Court of Religion.

The common monument of all Christendom, the Church of the Holy Sepulchre, is a building of a different character. About the main shrine, which is covered by a black dome, are ranged the chapels and crypts of each particular sect and community. Crowds of pilgrims continually pass to and fro shepherded by the monks or priests of their sect. The ceiling and walls of the chapel are hung with innumerable golden and silver votive lamps; the precincts are noisy with the stalls of the traffickers in candles and images and holy souvenirs. And the courtyard of the church itself is occupied by a Turkish patrol with rifles, put there to keep order between the contending churches.

There has been much ill-informed criticism of the Zionist idea because of the alleged difficulty concerning the Holy Places, if Palestine were inhabited and administered by the Jewish people. How can the Christian States, it is said, allow the most sacred sites to be under Jewish control? It would seem sufficient answer that the Jews will have at least as much regard for those sites as the Turks, and in modern times at any rate the Moslems have given no reason for a Crusade against them by their treatment of monuments. Despite the Hellenistic emperors, despite the Romans, despite the Crusaders, and despite the monks, Palestine is and always will be a Semitic country.

The suggested difficulty of adjustment between Jew and Arab is somewhat more actual; but with wisdom and goodwill, it too should not be hard to solve. The Jews and Arabs are of one stock, and it requires only sympathetic interpretation to make that community of origin a real binding force between them. In Jerusalem especially the genius of the environment helps to a good understanding. Abraham, the father of the two branches of the race, is, next to Mohammed, the most revered teacher of Islam, and Hebron is his town and known indeed, after Abraham's attribute, as *El-Khalil*, the Friend. The Jaffa Gate, as the Franks call it, which opens on the road to

Hebron, is for the Arab "Bab-el-Khahil," the Gate of Abraham. The great popular feast again is the Nebi Musa, the day of the prophet Moses. The Arabs from all over the district gather in Jerusalem and troop out in gay fantasias on that day to the mountain overlooking the Dead Sea, which they insist is the burial-place of the prophet. The Mosque of Omar, the religious centre, is built on the site of the Temple of Solomon, which, for Islam as for Jewry, has beloved associations. Apart from the ethnical points of sympathy, a fundamental unity of feeling exists between Jew and Moslem. One incident in a synagogue in Jerusalem brought home to me vividly this underlying agreement of religious outlook. We were repeating at the end of the Day of Atonement the last solemn declaration of the day, "The Lord, He is God." The synagogue was opposite a mosque and as we uttered Israel's declaration of faith, a Muezzin appeared on the minaret calling the Moslems to evening prayer, and cried, "Allah (the Lord) is God; Allah is One." For two peoples to whom religion is the deepest element of social and intellectual life, that fundamental basis of agreement is the best guarantee of a fruitful union. During the golden age of Arabic civilisation, both in Bagdad and in Spain, Jews and Moslems lived in harmony and rivalled each other in literature and philosophy. If later there have been persecutions and intolerance, they have been due to the degeneration produced by barbaric incursions. The Turk indeed has not, for the most part, been harsh to the Jew, but he has ruined the development of spiritual life throughout the Empire, so that both Arabs and Jews beneath his sway have decayed. But a renascent Hebrew people and a renascent Arab people, who will arise after the war, will grow together in unity and share the common pride in the new destiny of the whole Semitic race, contributing again to the wealth of humanity. On the material side, moreover, a community of interest will strengthen the spiritual bond. The Arab Fellah or peasant needs Jewish energy and imagination; the Jew in Palestine needs Arab hardihood and experience, for the prosperous development of the country. The Arab population in the country is indeed very sparse; little more than a quarter of a million scattered over hundreds of miles. There is another quarter of a million in the towns which to-day looms large everywhere, save in Jerusalem, simply because it is the majority. But when organised Western immigration begins in earnest, the Arabs will be a comparatively small class. The talk about their having to leave their homes is folly. There will be room, rather, for an Arab immigration as well as a Jewish, when the wasted fruitful spaces are reclaimed and the robbers are put down, when the Negeb is cultivated to the river of Gaza, and the uplands of Gilead are redeemed from the destructive Bedouins.

During the Tripolitan war between Turkey and Italy, a striking document was published in Jerusalem which gave a glimpse of the influence which the Holy City, when conscious of its spiritual power and inspired by some great revolution of the soul, might exert on the world. It was an appeal for peace or arbitration signed by the heads of all the different religious bodies in the city. Mohammedan imams and Jewish rabbis, Greek Orthodox papas and Roman Catholic priests, Protestant and Armenian bishops, all put their names to the protest against war in the name of a common belief in the reign of Justice. The appeal fell on deaf ears. The outer world was not yet attuned to the new message. But side by side with the League of the Nations to enforce peace, which is destined to be one of the great outcomes of the world war, there is a call for a League of the Religions, to foster peace among the peoples. Jerusalem has far older and more historical claims than the Hague or Washington to be the centre of the world's peace movement, and the Temple Mount would be the ideal spot for a sanctuary which should mark this new harmony moving the nations.

The prophet Zechariah looking for the

coming of the golden age 2,500 years ago, pictures Jerusalem without its walls, no longer a fortress but spread village-wise: "Jerusalem will be inhabited without walls for the multitude of men and cattle therein. For I, saith the Lord, will be to her a wall of fire round about, and will be the glory in the midst of her" (Zech. ii. 5). Another prophet of Jerusalem foretold the day when nation shall no longer lift up sword against nation, neither shall they learn war any more: "And the mountain of the Lord's house shall be established on the tops of the mountains, and shall be exalted above the hills, and all nations shall flow into it" (Isaiah ii. 2–4). The Jews are peculiarly fitted in our day to be the missionaries of peace, as they were once the missionaries of justice, because they have pre-eminently the international mind and the sense of a divine unity embracing the whole.

Disraeli used to insist that the Jew represented in Europe the Semitic principle—"all that is spiritual in our system"—and that it was his function to be the world's spiritual teacher. In exile and dispersion his function has been cramped and almost forgotten; back in his own land only can he revive it to fresh triumphs.

When the Holy City is the home, not only of religious fervour, but also of the progressive idealism which the Jew will bring with him from every hearth of thought, it will be the spiritual metropolis of mankind as the Hebrew seers conceived it : " And the Lord shall be King over all the earth. In that day shall the Lord be One and His name One."

CHAPTER VI

THE "HOLY CITIES" AND SEA OF GALILEE

THE most beautiful part of Palestine scenically, without a doubt, is Galilee. It is a country of green hills and green valleys which roll up from the plain of Esdraelon to the snowy mountains of Lebanon. It reaches its greatest beauty by the shores of the Lake, known as the Sea of Galilee, through which the Jordan flows in full and rapid stream. Of the Lake the Rabbis said: "God has created the seas, but Galilee is His particular delight." In Jewish story it is known as the Sea of the Harp (*Kinnereth*) because of its shape, and its waters are set like silver threads in a framework of purple mountains.

But from the Great Sea on the west to this land-locked Sea, and beyond to the plateau of the Hauran, and from hoary Hermon towering in the north to the comeliness of Mount Tabor that stands sentinel over the plain of Esdraelon in the south, the whole province is fair and verdant. Water is abundant and trees flourish wherever man chooses to plant them. Even to-day after a thousand years of neglect the ground in the spring is a carpet of wild flowers, a garden of nature.

The Jewish historian, Josephus, who was sent to defend the province against the Romans in the second century, thus rhapsodises: "The country that lies over against this lake bears the same name of Gennesareth. Its nature is wonderful, as well as its beauty; and its soil is so fruitful that all sorts of plants can grow in it, and the inhabitants do accordingly plant all sorts. For the temper of the air is so well mixed that it agrees very well with their several sorts, particularly walnuts, which require cold air, flourish there in abundance; there are palm trees also which grow but in hot air, fig trees also and olives grow near them which yet require an air that is more temperate. We may call the place the reconciliation of Nature, when it forces these plants that are naturally enemies of one another to agree together. It has a happy contention of the seasons as if each of them laid claim to the country. It supplies men with the principal fruits, with grapes and figs continually throughout the year, and with other fruit in their season" (*Wars*, iii. 8).

Galilee was originally the territory of Asher, Zebulon, Naphtali, and Issachar. The blessing of Asher betokening the abundance of the olive trees in his land was: "Let him dip his foot in oil." And of him it was said again, "His oil flows like a river." When the

Kingdom of Israel was taken into captivity, the territory of the four tribes was occupied by the surrounding peoples, and thenceforth the population was mixed between Hebrews and Gentiles. The country east of the Jordan was known particularly as "Galilee of the Gentiles" because of the preponderance of the heathen settlers. The Maccabæan princes conquered both parts of the country and converted the inhabitants to Judaism, and they settled there Judæans from the south. The mountainous homes nourished an ardent and impulsive population. For more than a century before the final catastrophe of the Jewish nation, the rebels fought here unceasingly against Roman tyranny. Galilee was the stronghold and the hearth of Jewish nationalism. The Romanising priests who were powerful about Jerusalem and Judæa had little hold among the Northern Highlanders. The Gospel of St. Matthew records how the part of Israel's kingdom which had first succumbed to the Assyrian invaders became the citadel of the Jewish religious revolt: "The land of Zebulon and the land of Naphtali, by the way of the Sea beyond Jordan, Galilee of the Gentiles. The people who dwelt in darkness saw a great light" (Matt. iv. 15).

In those days Galilee was a densely populated country. Its name means "a ring" or circle, and was given to it because of the ring of villages which the hills embraced. Alexander the Great after his conquest of the East planted settlements of Greeks near the lake, where Nature had invited men to dwell, and strategy required the guarding of the great military road fron Egypt to Sinai. The Ptolemies and Seleucids, who in turn ruled Palestine, followed his precedent, and an independent league of ten Greek cities in Galilee, Gilead, and the Hauran—the famous Decapolis—was constituted to maintain Hellenism. The Roman policy was to support the independence of the League against the Jewish Kingdom. Josephus writing in the first century of the Christian era speaks of 200 villages in Galilee of which the smallest contained 15,000 inhabitants. Allowing for the exaggeration of a writer who never regarded truth as sufficiently impressive, it is certain that when Jesus was preaching the land contained several large cities besides many considerable villages. The ruins of Tiberias on the west bank and of Kerak at the southern end of the Lake, the massive marble foundations of the synagogue at Tell-Hum (identified somewhat dubiously with Capernaum) and the striking relics of other places of worship in the Greek style which have been excavated among the hills round Safed, confirm the story. The Romanising Jewish historian tells too of various strong places which it took the Roman armies more than a year of hard warfare to capture, Tarichea and Gischala,

Magdala and Sepphoris, all mountainous fastnesses.

After Titus and Trajan and Hadrian had in turn devastated Judæa and driven out the Jews from their last stronghold in the south, Galilee became for centuries the chief seat of the national life, shorn of its political independence and of the colleges which preserved the full vigour of that life. The schools of Sepphoris and Jabne gave the law to all Jewry, and the Mishna, the crystallisation of the oral law, was written down in Tiberias. But Galilee at this period continued to be a great centre of Græco-Roman life, and the City of the Lake was as famous among the Roman nobles for its hot springs and its pleasures as it was among the Jewish congregations for its rabbis and jurists. There Greek merchants plied their commerce, caravans came jingling from Egypt and Persia and Mesopotamia, and the life within the town was as bright as the life of Nature without.

It was in this sunny atmosphere that the sages of the Talmud developed their wisdom, and the bright colouring of the Hagada and the homiletical literature doubtless owes much to their environment. Though the glory of the Kingdom was gone, the beauty of the land remained an inspiration. When, however, Christianity became imperial, and tyrants professing the new faith mounted the throne of Rome, the Jewish people were driven from

Galilee as from the rest of Palestine. Small communities found their way back whenever the enemies of the Christianised Roman Empire prevailed, but the resettlement was short-lived; the hegemony of the Galilean schools was gone and passed over to Mesopotamia.

During the existence of the Latin Kingdom of Jerusalem (1099–1291 C.E.) Galilee was full of the Crusaders' strongholds which were built to protect the Christian fiefs from the incursions of the Arab armies of Damascus. It was at the Horns of Hattin, overlooking Tiberias, that Saladin destroyed the flower of Western chivalry and gave the death-blow to that kingdom. The Saracen victor restored the right of the Jews to live in Palestine, prompted thereto by his Court physician, Maimonides. The body of the great Jewish physician and philosopher was buried at Tiberias. But the hordes of Asiatic barbarians who during the next 200 years overran the East, cut short the hope of a revival. It was not till the fifteenth century that Jewish life was again securely established in Galilee. Some thousands of the exiles from Spain and Portugal, driven out of the Peninsula by the Inquisition, made their way to Turkey, which was then the one tolerant power in Europe. They settled in different parts of the Ottoman Empire and soon made their way to Palestine, and they established a new seat of learning and law at Safed. That town is not mentioned by name in the Bible, though certain scholars have identified it with the "city set on a hill" of the New Testament. A legend, however, of the early centuries of the civil era had it that the Messiah will spring thence, and its neighbourhood was celebrated in the annals of Jewish resistance to Rome and of Rabbinical mysticism. It took the precedence in favour of all the historical sites of Northern Palestine, and the fame of some of the early settlers set the seal on its popularity.

Jewish mediæval scholarship and philosophy had reached their zenith shortly before the expulsion from Spain, and in the sixteenth century, Safed, continuing the work of the Spanish sages, had its golden age and became the chief university of Jewish learning in the world. It was then, as Schechter describes it, "a city of legists and cryptics." For Jewish literature at the time had two main streams: the development and codification of the legal traditions, and devotional writings directed to the inner mysteries of religion. It was in Safed that Joseph Caro wrote in 1542 his famous Jewish Corpus the *Beth Joseph*, his popular abridgment of which, the *Shulchan Aruch*, is still accepted as the authoritative legal and ritual code of orthodox Jewry. It was in Safed, too, that Isaac Luria (1534–1572), gathering around him a body of disciples, founded the modern school of the *Kabbala*—the traditional lore or sacred mystery.

A little later on an endeavour of a different kind was made to restore the Jews to their ancient soil. Don Joseph of Naxos, a Jewish diplomatist at the Ottoman Court, who was sprung from a Spanish-Jewish family and had achieved a commanding position with the Sultan, obtained as a reward for his services, a Firman, sanctioning a Jewish settlement in Galilee. His attempt at land colonisation was made shortly after the collapse of the movement of the false Messiah, Sabbatai Zevi; and the man of affairs aspired to do by practical means what the man of miracles had failed to do by appeals to the supernatural. Don Joseph died before the scheme was fully developed and left no successor. But some hundreds of Jewish families were planted on the soil in the hill country, and their descendants remain to this day still working as peasants on the land. Lord Kitchener when surveying Northern Palestine was amazed to come across them in Pekah and other villages in this district. By faith and feature alike they were different from the Arab peasants, and, on the other hand, in physique and habit they were distinguishable from the Jews of the neighbouring towns of Tiberias and Safed. They represent a genuine Jewish peasant class, with a title to their homesteads of more than two centuries. A century ago earthquake and fire laid Safed in ruins and reduced the once flourishing Holy City to little more than a holy village; and the work of Joseph of Naxos was not taken up again till the modern development of Jewish colonisation.

The nineteenth century saw a large increase of the Jewish town-dwelling population of Galilee. Tiberias and Safed became again predominantly Jewish towns. In the former there are not fewer than 8,000 Jews out of a total of 12,000; in the latter 10,000 out of 15,000 inhabitants. But the greater numbers have not brought another Golden Age of learning. There are Talmudical schools by the score, but no famous scholars spring from them; and the conditions under which most of the people live are extremely wretched. In both places man has contrived perversely to spoil Nature. Only a few ruins to-day suggest the Græco-Roman splendour of the one place, the mediæval and more recent fame of the other. Part of the Saracen walls and the castle of Tiberias are still standing. But within the walls to-day is a mass of huddled dwellings, dirty and ruinous. The only buildings worthy of the name are the Serail, or Government office, two missionary schools, a hospital, and the German hotel. Kinglake sixty years ago marked the place as the residence of the King of the Fleas, and the dynasty is still in possession. The market, such as it is, is the rendezvous of the Jewish pedlars of the district, who, when not engaged in business, are also pietists. The one sign of modernity about the place is the motor-boats which an enterprising firm has started to run between Samach, the station on the Hedjaz line at the south end of the Lake, and the town. There are a number of stout fishing boats in the port and on the lake, such as doubtless were used by the apostles nearly 2,000 years ago The hot springs which made the fortune of Tiberias among the Græco-Roman society are still frequented locally, but, like everything else in the place, they are half ruinous. The bath-house is an ordinary domed structure and the bathing is free, but there is a private bath supplied by a separate spring for the use of which a small charge, a beshlik (half-franc), is made. In time a great Sanatorium will arise here which will bring a fortune to its undertakers, and revive perhaps the old popularity of the district.

The way from Tiberias to Safed lies along the banks of the lake to its northern edge and then westwards over the hills till you finally come to the mountain, 3,000 feet high, on the flank of which the city lies. Along the banks of the lake the road passes the Russo-Jewish colony of MEJDEL (Magdala of the New Testament) and close by is the settlement of *Tapcha* (reputed, doubtfully, to be the ancient Tarichea), where the German Templars of last century tried to establish an agricultural settlement. A single home, a luxuriant garden, and a few fertile fields now constitute their domain, for most of their colonists died in this malarial paradise. Mejdel also was a foundation of their society which had to be abandoned. The Jewish colonising societies have been more prudent; experience has taught them that before these long abandoned marshlands can again become populous, man must clear and drain the overflowing vegetation of a too luxurious nature. " Sanity of sanities, all is sanitation," is the note of the modern colonisers.

Clustered along the mountain slopes, and fanned in all seasons of the year by the breezes of the Lebanon, SAFED should be a garden city celebrated for its healthiness. In actual fact, it is a byword even in Palestine for congestion with all its concomitant evils. At a distance it is a vision of romantic loveliness comparable with Taormina in Sicily, but when you reach the place you find, as in many another Sicilian or Italian place of beauty, a baffling maze of squalid alleys which a single donkey makes almost impassable, and of squalid hovels which provide a doubtful shelter for their occupants. One refinement of civilisation had indeed come to Safed before the war: a public water supply laid on from a spring in the hills. Seventeen public fountains were set up in the various quarters of the town. This remarkable innovation was due to a progressive Kaimakam (or Prefect)—a Moslem-Arab, active and shrewd and ambitious, and with some ideas of modern municipal development. He also was responsible for the planning of a road to Tiberias. He told me when I visited him in 1911 that in both of these enterprises his chief help came from the Jews. He complained of the inadequate support which he got from the Town Council, which was elected by Ottoman subjects paying a certain amount of tax. Most of the Jews were Uitlanders, and had no voice. He had some ideas about the weaknesses of popular government in an uneducated people like the Arabs and Turks; and he was in favour of granting the vote to foreign subjects because they were more progressive than the Arabs. It was an unfortunate feature of the Turkish régime that when a good Governor appeared once in a way, he was moved on before his work was half done, either as a reward for his success or as a warning against too much energy. The progressive Kaimakam of Safed did not stay long, and the sanitation of Safed remains a task for the future administration.

Apart from its public water supply Safed has little enough to boast of in the way of material civilisation. Nor is it rich any more in spiritual goods. It is of the degenerate type of Holy City; an obsolete relic of mediæval piety almost extinct, unaffected by new ideas. The outer and inner conditions of life are at one, but both are in decay.

Mediævalism, however insanitary, is at least picturesque, and the narrow lanes of Safed are attractive with their medley of peoples and manners; Arabs, in their yellow and red and many-coloured head-scarves and sheepskins, jostling with rabbis or students in their black velvet hats and dark kaftans; peasant women bringing their baskets of fruit and vegetables, or carrying on their heads trays of chickens or leading sheep; and Jewish women chattering and haggling in the shops. On the seventh day of the week, for the sake of which, according to a pretty saying, the other six are created, a genuine holiness transforms the place. As in Heine's legend the Jewish pedlar on the Sabbath eve becomes a prince, so on the Sabbath in Safed the hovel becomes a home. The Sabbath is welcomed with the joy and love with which the groom meets his bride. The father of the family dons his silk and plush robe, his wife's wedding gift, and his fur-trimmed strummel, an inappropriate but decorative costume; his wife wears her white gown and silken shawl; the little living-room is beautified by the white cloth, the Sabbath lights and the invisible spirit of the Sabbath; the Ghetto streets are quiet save for the sound of singing, and the outskirts, as far as the stretched boundary of the Sabbath-day journey, are frequented by an almost merry throng. On the other days, morning, noon, and eve the young boys are gathered in the Talmud Torahs, where they learn only Jewish lore, and that in Yiddish or Ladino. The older boys and men of all ages are gathered in the Yesheboths (seminaries), where they con for hours together the Rabbinical literature, and spin the subtleties of ritual jurisprudence. Here and there a new spiritual force is thrown off, a student of genius becomes a real teacher—but he leaves Safed. The director of Jewish education in New York and the chief Rabbis of Constantinople and Salonica were children of Safed whose intelligence was sharpened in its schools, their native energy being left, by a miracle, unimpaired. It must be difficult indeed to escape from the evil canker which afflicts the general community.

Pauperism is a skilled profession here, practised by a whole army of scribes and collectors and distributors who thrive on the debasement of the beautiful idea that the Jewish people, though debarred from the contact of the land, should possess in their ancestral home a remnant to keep alive the tradition of learning. By the system known as the *Chaluka* (distribution) the Jewish communities of the Diaspora were united to contribute, by a kind of voluntary taxation, a fund for the maintenance of the schools in Palestine. This fund was divided among the representatives resident in the Holy Cities of the communities contributing. When I visited Safed there were twenty-one *Kolelim* (communities) each with a separate Chaluka fund and separate, and rival, staffs of missioners, scribes, and distributors. Some represented countries, others single towns. Middlemen in Europe and America intercept a large part of the fund, and according to report the beneficiaries receive little more than a quarter of what has been contributed. The petty jealousies and intrigues of a Barchester Close are multiplied in this Ghetto. Petitions wander the world over asking for help and composed in queer English, or more doubtful French, and dithyrambic Yiddish or Hebrew. With a little encouragement the emissaries will denounce the Chaluka system and confess its defects; but they plead they are powerless agents in it, caught themselves in the wheels of its relentless machinery. In Safed anyway it is powerful and unchallenged, as Tammany Hall is in New York.

The school of the Alliance Israélite has introduced the elements of a more independent life and outlook; the boys and girls who are its pupils are taught to earn their living in other ways and, through the same influence, some touch of modernism is beginning to invade the dead piety and rampant beggary of the place. The war which is acting as the great sweeper away of cobwebs in all parts will sweep away, too, the spirit of the Ghetto from Safed, and when the larger Jewish immigration comes there, as come it will, the new energy will submerge the old passivism with all the evils that have followed from it. The Hebrew school has already freed the younger generation of Jerusalem from the taint of the Chaluka; it will free likewise the younger generation of these Holy Cities of the north.

A few miles outside Safed is *Meiron*, the most famous of Jewish pilgrimage places, where Rabbi Simeon ben Yochai, one of the great mystics of the Roman period and the reputed father of the Kabbalah, lived and died. Simeon certainly did not compose the *Zohar*, the Book of Light, which is the second Bible of the Kabbalists. But he has been venerated as the perfect sage, the patron saint of the Chassidim, the righteous. From the days of Ezekiel to the present time pious mysticism has formed an integral part of the Jewish consciousness. In the Dark Ages, which extended for the homeless people from the thirteenth to the eighteenth century, the Jews assimilated the religious weaknesses, as to-day they tend to assimilate the national weaknesses, of their environments. Holy sites and the tombs of holy men became objects of veneration to them as well as to Moslems and Christians. The fame of the schools of Safed served to increase the fame of the old shrines in its neighbourhood; and while to visit Jerusalem was the desire of every Jew, to visit Meiron was the special object of the followers of the Kabbalah.

The great day of the pilgrimage was the thirty-third day of the *Omer* (the days of counting between Passover and Pentecost), which is known as the Scholars' Feast. Bands came together for that anniversary from Eastern Europe and Central Asia, from Persia and Salonica, which were all centres of the Kabbalistic schools; and on the festal day itself they danced, and jumped through fire, and were carried away in frenzied ecstasy. Oliphant, a mystic himself, has described the scene in his *Letters from Haifa*, observing: "The Jewish pilgrim has the same intense faith as the Russian peasants who assemble in the Church of the Sepulchre at Easter to catch the Holy Fire." The pilgrimage is still observed on the traditional day, with some of the old traditional rites. At other times Meiron is remarkable only as the site of a big college, or rather two colleges, one for the Ashkenazi ritual Jews and the other for the Sephardim. The traditional Synagogue of Ben Yochai is a Hellenistic ruin, lying higher up on the mountain; and, on the hill beyond, another ruined synagogue of the Hellenistic period still witnesses, with its marble columns and pillars, to the beauty and the wealth that endured while the national life lasted. A little further along is the hamlet of Gis, covering the site of the historical Gishala, which was one of the fortresses that the Zealots held against Vespasian and Titus. From the mountain crags one surveys the whole of green Galilee and looks up to snowy Hermon and Lebanon in the north, to the cornfields of the Hauran on the east, and to the blue peaceful water of the Mediterranean, bordered by the white clusters of Acre, Sidon, and Tyre, on the west.

It is not strange that those who dwelt on these heights and had these views continually before them, should have fought with desperate heroism to preserve their land from Roman domination. They were freemen of the mountains, and had the love of liberty which the Swiss and the Highlanders everywhere have shown. To-day it is still manifestly a land worth fighting for, and in those days its fertility and attractiveness were multiplied manifold. Gishala means "a clot of oil," and the name was given to the place because of its wealth of olive groves. To-day the hillsides to the west of Safed are bare and treeless save where the little Jewish colony of *Ain-Zeitun* (the Spring of the Olives) arises in a green oasis in the midst of the limestone rock. On the other side of Safed, where the hills slope down to Jordan, groves are more frequent and cover the grass for miles. The planting of forests is among the greatest needs of Palestine. The Turkish Government by putting a tax on every tree discouraged what is essential to the prosperity of the country. "The oak scorns to grow except on free ground" was the old English adage when, under the system of copyhold tenure, the lord of the manor could take for himself the best of the timber planted by his tenant. Similarly the Arabs have a saying: "The olive has not time to grow in the Turkish Empire." Before it can be firmly rooted it is taxed out of existence. A wiser administration would give a bonus, instead of imposing a tax, for every tree planted; and then the olive groves of Galilee would be as famous as the orange groves of Jaffa.

North of Safed and the Lake of Galilee the country becomes more and more mountainous as it approaches the towering white crest of Mount Hermon. Water is abundant. The gorge of the Litany river and the headlong streams that make the beginning of the Jordan, are very different from the rivers of Southern Palestine, more like torrents that dash out from the Alps. New Jewish villages, *Yesod-Hamaaleh*, *Mishmar Ha-Jarden* (Guard of the Jordan) by the reed-crowned waters of Meron (Lake Huleh), and Metullah, perched on the very edge of Lebanon, are at present the only settlements in this lovely region of Northern

Galilee. The Hauran and Gilead await a strong government, and a devoted population, to bring back the old fertility. The Greek ruins of Banias, the ancient Dan, which changed its name when the temple of the Greek god Pan was erected there, give a suggestion of the splendour and spaciousness of the town which was the chief city of a province. It was one of the places on which the Herods, of barbaric origin, lavished their outward show of Hellenisation. The strategical importance of the site doubtless induced them to disguise the fortress in the setting of a pleasure city; for Banias is the natural frontier stronghold of Palestine. Its position at the entrance of the defile between Mount Lebanon and Mount Hermon has been compared to that of Peshawur, at the entrance of the Khyber Pass between India and Afghanistan. The source of the Jordan here rushes out from the gorge, and, according to ancient legend, the river takes its name from two streams Jor and Dan which here unite. The abundance of waters has preserved a luxuriant wood even after hundreds of years of neglect. And beyond are the pine-clad slopes of Hermon and another land—Syria.

On the coast which fringes Galilee two of the world's most ancient havens for ships, *Tyre* and *Sidon*, were famous at the time of the Homeric wars, and were the mother-cities of the Phœnician people. They owe their ancient pride to the rocky promontories which at either place jut out from the mainland and form an anchorage on each side for ships. Tyre was the Liverpool of the old world; the principal port from which bold men sailed to the West and brought back the goods of the civilised world. Sidon was second only to Tyre. To-day their anchorages are still filled with fishing and sailing vessels, but larger ships must lie some way out. What were the marts of the East are now fishing villages. The strand, framed with its orange groves and its white clustered houses, is still a lovely Riviera. Palestine will certainly never lack an outlet for its trade. Along that short line of coast there are dotted six historical ports, Gaza, Jaffa, Haifa, Acre, Tyre, and Sidon. Each was a centre of commerce in the Hellenistic and the Roman epochs; each was a fortress in the Middle Ages; each may be a port and trading place again when the land in the interior is made fruitful once more by the toil of man. The stuffs of Phœnicia were famous in the commerce of a thousand years before the Christian era, and the purple shell which gave the Tyrian dye is still gathered on the beach. And one of the chief glories of the Constantinople museum is the sarcophagus, entitled of Alexandra the Great, which was unearthed at Sidon. By the great decorativeness of its sculpture it shows how art was developed here in the Hellenistic period of Eastern history. The Jews will succeed to the Phœnicran, as well as the Hebraic, heritage when they return to their own country.

What an industrious population and a tolerable administration may do in restoring the ancient populousness and fertility of the land, is illustrated in the Lebanon province immediately to the north of Galilee. Fifty years ago that was as neglected and empty a country as Galilee or Gilead. But since the fierce feud between Maronites and Druses which led, on the intervention of France, to the grant to the Province of a semi-autonomous constitution, the Syrian Christians have been able to administer their affairs with only a limited amount of obstruction from the Turkish authorities, and there has been continuous progress. The density of the population has been increased fourfold, the soil has been reclaimed to rich cultivation, great broad hard roads have been built over the Lebanon passes, large villages with unlimited water supply and lit up with electricity have grown up on the hill-sides. *Beirut*, from a fishing village comparable with Sidon and Tyre, has to-day again become one of the chief ports of the Mediterranean, with a fair harbour and 150,000 inhabitants, and it has revived its ancient status of a University town, which it enjoyed under the Romans. The college of the Jesuits and the Anglo-American mission are the principal seats of learning of the whole of the Syrian people. The Syrians, in fact, through the enjoyment of a little autonomy and the appeal to their national pride have done on a large scale in their country what the Jewish settlers have done in miniature in Palestine.

Give the Jews in Palestine the same opportunity as the Syrians have had in the northern province and the world will see, and wonder perhaps at the sight, for how short a time Judæa will remain barren, Galilee neglected, and Gilead deserted. When a larger body of immigrants from the free lands of the West have been brought in and established in settlements over the whole land, then Galilee will be again a ring of cities rising from wooded heights, of villages set amid smiling cornfields and olive groves, covered as it was in the past with roads—roads from the harbours of Phœnicia to Samaria, the Hauran, and Damascus, roads from Sharon to the valley of the Jordan, roads from the sea to the desert —the smiling province of a prosperous land, the pride of Israel the world over.

CHAPTER VII

THE RENAISSANCE IN THE SCHOOLS

In describing his ideal "Republic," Plato discusses at the outset the form of education which shall be given to its citizens. In order that they may maintain the new order, his guardians must have a new system of moral and intellectual training, based on a more perfect psychology than was current in the Athenian schools of his day. The reform of society which the philosopher contemplates, is pre-eminently to be brought about by a reform of education, without which no political revolution can work any lasting good. "Even as the twig is bent, so is the tree inclined." The converse of the same idea is conveyed in the saying of a rabbi that the Jewish nation was destroyed because the mothers of Israel had ceased to teach their children the study of the Law. So, in our own time, it may be said that Judaism is in danger because of the neglect of that study. The deeper evils from which the Jews of the West suffer to-day, religious indifference, materialism, and a soulless assimilation, are the direct outcome of a bad, or defective, Jewish education. The creation of a new spirit must be initiated in the schools. In the ghettoes of Eastern Europe, where Jews have been ruthlessly cut off from a free and full development of life, and their economic position is inconceivably wretched, Jewish education tends inevitably to be narrow and one-sided. In the cities of Western Europe, on the other hand, where Jewish life has continually to struggle against the compelling attraction of non-Jewish culture, religious teaching tends to be more and more neglected and to be crowded out of the child's education. The development of a sound knowledge of Judaism is almost impossible, and at the best the Jewish part of the child's training is a compromise. If anywhere the growth of a healthier system may be looked for it is in Palestine, where Jews already live neither in a cramping ghetto nor amid a foreign culture, and where they have begun to found a proper home—*ex Oriente lux*.

Every variety of Jewish school is to be seen in Palestine to-day. There are, in the first place, the schools of the ghetto—the Cheder, and the old-fashioned Talmud Torah. The Jews, it has been said, have carried into every country of the exile a moral Palestine. But it is equally true that the Jews have brought back with them into Palestine something of the spirit of the exile. The greater part of the earlier Jewish inhabitants of the Holy Land came there from Eastern Europe, led by motives of piety to study, to pray, and to mourn for the sorrows of Israel. Dwelling for the most part in the four holy cities, as they are called—Jerusalem, Hebron, Tiberias, and Safed—places stored with venerable Jewish associations from the ancient and middle ages, they have brought to them the economic conditions, the costume, the language, and the manners of the European ghetto, all of which ill befit their surroundings. There is no scope for petty trading; the climate makes kaftans and fur hats absurd; Yiddish is an anomaly; and the Cheder and Talmud Torah, in which Yiddish is the language of instruction, and the subjects and system of teaching are mediæval, are anachronisms. But all these things must live on for a time. The old-fashioned Cheder and the Talmud Torah in the Palestinian towns are like the Cheder and Talmud Torah elsewhere, save only that here they provide the whole education of the pupils. There is no rival secular school, and the great majority of the parents will not let their children go to the Christian Missionary School, which is anxious to receive them. In the Cheder the teacher instructs in a little room a number of boys, ranging from ten to eighty, in couples or threes, while the rest con their lessons or repeat aloud what they have just learnt. His chief qualification is that he has none for any other vocation. In the Talmud Torah more approach is made to educational method. The pupils, who are more numerous, are divided into classes; some syllabus of instruction is drawn up, and the *Melammedim* (teachers) have to satisfy a managing Committee as to their Hebrew knowledge and religious orthodoxy. Other educational qualifications are not often demanded and are rarely forthcoming. In both Cheder and Talmud Torah the teaching is imparted through Yiddish, and the chief subjects of instruction are the Bible and its commentaries, and Talmud. Modern subjects are altogether ignored, and the excellence aimed at is the knowledge of the Rabbinical literature. Finally, little provision is made for the teaching of girls in this old type of school.

It was to remedy the economic evils and intellectual deficiencies which this system of education is calculated to perpetuate, that the Jews of Western Europe established during the latter half of last century a new kind of school in Palestine. A deep sentiment for the revival of Jewish life in the Holy Land moved the newly emancipated Jewries at that period. Under the influence of inspiring leaders like Crémieux and Moses Montefiore, the prosperous Jews of the West, recognising that " All Israel is responsible the one for the other," manifested a strong feeling of fraternity with the struggling Jews of the East, and founded associations for their assistance. The French Alliance Israélite Universelle, followed by the Anglo-Jewish Association and the Hilfsverein der Deutschen Juden, provided in the towns of Palestine, as well as in other parts of the Orient, schools conducted according to modern ideas of education, for girls as well as for boys. But while these schools served a common purpose, each was, to some extent, designed according to the educational ideas of the country of the founding body, and aimed at instilling the ideas of that country into its pupils. To this end teachers were sent out from France, England, and Germany, and the teaching, naturally enough, was given in the native language of the teachers. The division of languages is the besetting problem of education in the heterogeneous societies of the Orient; but the method of teaching the children three or four tongues, and all through a language different from that of the home, is not a happy solution. It sacrifices preciseness of speech and vigour of thought; for scarcely any can think clearly save in the mother tongue, and to speak in a foreign language is as cramping as to compose on a typewriter.

The founders of the Alliance Schools, Crémieux and Netter, had indeed an intense Jewish feeling, and were eager to foster a living Jewish culture in Palestine, but their successors did not inherit their enthusiasm,

RENAISSANCE IN THE SCHOOLS

and allowed this part of their ideal to be submerged. The course of instruction was made to embrace the subjects which form part of the ordinary elementary education in the schools of Western Europe, and in some cases extended to a technical training to fit the pupil for a trade or handicraft. Hebrew and religious knowledge were, of course, part of the curriculum, but in the schools of the Alliance they took a secondary place, and the standard of attainment in them was low. The Alliance for long maintained the largest number of the European schools in Palestine. Besides a number of elementary schools, it supported at Jaffa and at Jerusalem technical workshops and it had the management of the agricultural college, *Mikveh Israel* (the Hope of Israel), which, as has been already noted, was the pioneer institution of the later agricultural settlement.

By a certain irony of circumstances the Jewish community which was most thoroughly assimilated and most completely denationalised —the community of Paris—played for a long period the largest part in the educational organisation of the Jewish population of Palestine. The French schools were exotic; and even when they started with some genuine Jewish enthusiasm, this was soon lost in an overgrowth of foreign influence. The *Mikveh Israel* College, which was founded by Charles Netter in 1876, was at the outset dominated by the strong Jewish sympathies of its founder, who had an ardent passion to bring the Jewish people back as cultivators to their old land. But when he died in 1882 the enthusiasm died with him, and for thirty years the school directorate opposed the national longing of the Palestinian young men, and became more and more estranged from popular feeling and less effective for its special function. It is significant of the growing strength of the national consciousness in Palestine that, in the year preceding the war, the Alliance replaced their Frenchifying director by a man who was in full sympathy with the new Hebraism, and who, having spent many years in superintending some of the colonies in Galilee, could appeal to the young generation of the Yishub.

The same foreign atmosphere for a time pervaded the Alliance schools in the agricultural colonies, which are scattered about the plains and hills of Palestine. When the colonies received the doubtful benefit of a French administration each large settlement was equipped with a modern elementary school. And while the whole environment called for a specifically Jewish culture of the mind, the tendency of the Alliance was still to establish a French village school with a Western outlook. It was inevitable that a school of this character, subordinating as it did traditional Jewish learning to practical subjects, should not satisfy the religious spirit of many of the settlers; and side by side with the official school in the larger colonies, a Talmud Torah sprang up, perpetuating by its Yiddish and its neglect of secular knowledge, amid the healthier Jewish life upon the land, something of the cramped spirit of the ghetto.

The Alliance schools have at times been put in *Cherem* (excommunication) by the most orthodox section of the community, and when they were built prayers were offered at the Wailing Wall for the preservation of Jerusalem from a new danger. None the less, they have usually attracted as many children as they could accommodate, and they have conferred some benefits on their pupils which their severest critics will not deny. They have inculcated habits of discipline, order, and neatness; they have done much for the general uplifting of the girls, whose education had hitherto been almost entirely neglected and whose social position was consequently degraded; and they have trained a large number of young men and women to useful occupations and saved them from the taint of pauperism and the demoralisation of idleness. But at the same time it is clear that they tended to encourage the young men and women to emigrate from Palestine and make their living in the West rather than in the East, to break down the religious loyalty of the younger generation, and to set up foreign ideas and fashions as the universal standard. The Alliance teachers carried to an extreme the alien influence, the foreign outlook, and the exhibition of the least regard for the traditions of the people for whose mental and moral equipment they were called on to provide.

The Anglo-Jewish Association, which is wholly responsible for one school only, the Evelina de Rothschild foundation for girls at Jerusalem, has shown, on the other hand, greater adaptability to the local conditions, and paid much greater regard to the feelings of the people. A strong religious tone pervades the instruction, and nothing perhaps marks more strikingly the Hebraic revival in Jerusalem than the recognition of Hebrew as a living language at this important school, where till recently the teaching was imparted through English. Now the children learn to speak both Hebrew and English, and with that bright intellect which seems to flower even more in the East than in the West, they speak and write both equally well.

The German-Jewish philanthropic association, the Hilfsverein der Deutschen Juden, for a time also conceded much to the growing national spirit. But a year before the outbreak of war, with what seemed then inexplicable blindness, but now appears to have been the prompting of some political influence, its directors attempted to reverse this sound policy. Devoting itself largely to the education of the younger children, the Hilfsverein had established kindergartens in the towns which had a considerable Jewish population, Jerusalem, Jaffa, Haifa, Tiberias, Safed, and Hebron, and also in the larger villages. It had in addition assumed the direction in Jerusalem of the Von Lamel Secondary School for boys, which was founded in the sixties, and it had opened a Teachers' Normal College, also in Jerusalem, in order to meet the demand for trained teachers in the improved schools of the colonies. Further it was responsible for a girls' secondary school, a school of commerce, and a small Rabbinical Seminary, all in the same city. Finally, it had the direction, together with representatives of American and Russian Jewry and of the Zionist body, of a Technical Institute at Haifa which had not yet opened its courses. Hebrew was the only language in the kindergartens and a principal language of these other schools. The Hilfsverein had thus embarked for some years before the war on a large and comprehensive programme of educational work in Palestine, and it was rapidly becoming the dominant outside body. Its larger understanding of the wants of the people, and its greater readiness to enrol on its staff the popular leaders of thought among the settlers, made it a far stronger influence than the Alliance Israélite.

And it was the most powerful of all the foreign factors in the development of the renaissance of the Schools in Palestine.

What followed, however, is instructive and illuminating, for in 1913 the society suddenly aroused a violent storm of protest throughout the country by increasing the German element in the curriculum of the higher schools and making it the main language of instruction. At the same time, the Council of Management of the Haifa Polytechnic, on which the Hilfsverein members had a majority, passed a resolution that German should be the language both for technical and general subjects at the Modern school and at the Polytechnic, which was then nearing completion. The Haifa Institute, built on the slopes of Mount Carmel, at a cost of £100,000, was designed on a big scale and was to have departments of engineering, chemistry, and textile industries. It was the particular pride of Palestinian Jewry and was to play a great part, it was hoped, in the extension of manufactures and commerce throughout the country. A generous bequest of a Jewish merchant prince of Odessa had started the fund for the erection of the building, and the site was given by the Jewish National Fund. The Hilfsverein and some leading Jewish philanthropists of America had contributed large sums to the building and maintenance funds, and it was understood that, in accordance with the wishes of the people, Hebrew would be the principal language of instruction. The decision of the council therefore came as a shock to the Palestine communities, and together with the new policy in the higher schools evoked the greatest hostility. When protest meetings were ineffective to secure a change, the Hebrew-loving teachers proclaimed a strike. A large number of the children and of the teachers withdrew from the Hilfsverein schools and it was announced that, unless the decision as to language was changed, the Polytechnic would be boycotted. The people were feeling their independence of foreign help, and with an ardent love of their newly won language refused to bend the knee to any Teutonic Baal.

David Yellin, one of the leaders of the Hebrew revival and sub-director of the Teachers' Training College, resigned his post and put himself at the head of a movement for the establishing of independent Hebrew higher schools. Over £5,000 was subscribed for the purpose by the Western Zionists in a few months, and the people of Palestine, poor as most of them are, subscribed as much. The teachers willingly submitted to great material loss for the sake of their ideal, and the new schools were soon fully manned and fully attended. Nothing could better illustrate the spirit of the Palestine settlers than this bold championship of Hebrew, and this refusal to make concessions to any foreign influence, philanthropic though it might be, which challenged their national sentiment. The Polytechnic stood an empty fabric until the fiercer war outside came to resolve the struggle between the Teutonisers and these latter-day Maccabees. The school is the centre of Jewish life, and it was round the schools that the battle against foreign influence was waged, while it was the teachers who were to lead in the fight. What they aspired to, was a Hebrew people nurtured on a Hebraic foundation, and conscious of a national unity through their common Hebraism, instead of a collection of Russo-Jewish, Franco-Jewish, and German-Jewish atoms, and they proved by their conduct in this struggle with the powerful outside elements arrayed against them, their attachment to their ideals and their power to attain them.

For thirty years, Jewish life in Palestine did not evolve a system of education in harmony with the ideal which prompted the return to the land. It continued to foster through the Talmud Torah and the Cheder, on the one hand, the spirit of exile in the form of a petrifaction of Jewish thought; through the foreign schools, on the other hand, had the same spirit in the more insidious form of assimilation. The new spirit of the revival required a system based on Jewish traditional teaching free at once from the trammels of

RENAISSANCE IN THE SCHOOLS 165

the ghetto and the slavish adherence to Western models, while remaining in touch with the best modern science and European thought. Since the beginning of this century at least, Jewish education in Palestine has in fact advanced far along the lines of such a development.

While orators were talking Jewish nationalism in Europe, a few workers were fashioning it in Palestine. The enthusiasm for the revival of the Hebrew language was among the first expressions of the national consciousness of the people, and marvellously quickly it permeated the mass. Necessity was the sister force of enthusiasm; for a practical need supplemented the poetical sentiment. The immigrants spoke three or four languages in their homes, some the Yiddish of the European ghetto; some the Ladino or Spanish dialect which is spread among the Jews of the Levant; some Judeo-Arabic which is the native speech of the Orient. Hebrew was the single language which could give a corporate feeling to the mass of the younger generation, and it was therefore accepted by all but the very pious mediævalists, who continued to regard its use for secular purposes as a blasphemy. The Talmud Torah in the village gave place to the Beth-Hasepher, which was designed to foster a new Hebraism. Taking over the modern subjects which had been introduced in the foreign schools by European teachers, it taught them through Hebrew, and though defects of methods remain, and enough good teachers are difficult to find, on the whole the colonies and the larger towns have now an adequate system of elementary instruction imparted in Hebrew and inspired by Jewish feeling.

As Jewish life has expanded the educational demands have increased. The Jewish parent everywhere in Palestine, as well as in London, in Odessa, in New York, will make every sacrifice to give his child the best possible education ; and if it cannot be obtained near at hand, he will send the child abroad. Till recently most of the boys and girls who wanted a higher education, whether technical, professional, or artistic, left Palestine to seek it in Paris, or Berlin, or Switzerland. But apart from the foundations of foreign philanthropic societies, the popular movement has already brought about the establishment of several higher schools in Palestine itself ; notably the Gymnasium at Jaffa and the Bezalel Arts and Crafts School at Jerusalem, which are the spontaneous outcome of the new Jewish settlement, and in their methods and objects reflect its character.

The Hebrew Gymnasium at Jaffa was, up to the outbreak of the war, the special boast of the Jewish Garden City, TEL-AVIV ; what Harrow, at an earlier stage, was to the Metropolis. It was a high school for boys

RENAISSANCE IN THE SCHOOLS 167

and girls between the ages of twelve and seventeen, and it had already sent scholars to European universities. During the ten years of its existence the roll of its pupils rose from 100 to over 600, of whom about one half were drawn from Jaffa, Jerusalem, and the Agricultural colonies, and the other half from Southern Russia. The schools of Palestine were becoming the magnet of the Russian Jews, who could send but a small percentage of their children to higher schools in Russia itself, and were thus compelled to look to Western Europe before the new light began to shine in the East. But a Jewish Gymnasium in Jaffa was dearer to them far than a Swiss Gymnasium in Geneva, and a policy of restriction against the Russo-Jewish immigration had already begun to close the portals of the Western schools and universities. Through the generosity of an ex-Lord Mayor of Bradford, Alderman Moser, the Jaffa high schools were finely housed in a building which was one of the few architectural beauties of the town, standing in the centre of the Jewish suburb. The curriculum included Hebrew, Bible and Talmud, mathematics and natural science, Latin and Greek, Arabic and Turkish, French and English, singing and gymnastics. The list of the subjects is striking in its diversity, but the distinctive feature of the school was its method. Each of the lessons was given through Hebrew ; boys and girls were taught together. While in the ghetto the girls were neglected intellectually, in the new Judæa they were to have from the beginning equality of opportunity. The staff of the school was likewise partly male and partly female, and was drawn mostly from the class of the Russian intelligenzia. Definite religious teaching was avoided because of the difference in religious standpoint among parents and teachers. Jewish beliefs, in Palestine, as everywhere, are in process of transition; but there is nowhere else the Jewish environment, moulding the life of the people and compensating, to some extent, for a falling off in ceremonial observance

The question of religious teaching has been a vexed one with the Jews not less than with other peoples, both inside and outside Palestine. A section of the nationalists profess a complete secularism, while another section maintain a complete adherence to the religious tradition. Excess begets excess; and the minute regulation of life by religious law which exists in the ghettoes of Eastern Europe, produces among the newly emancipated a violent reaction against religious belief and practice. But in Palestine the *genius loci* makes, undoubtedly, for the growth of a religious feeling of a deeper kind. Many of the boys and girls of the Jaffa Gymnasium, having a good knowledge of the Bible and of the literature which grew up around the Bible, already show a fresh religious sense which is of good augury for the future Jewish life of the new settlement.

Besides its elementary and higher schools the Jaffa settlement boasted a Conservatoire of Music, the " Shulamith." Of all the arts, music has the deepest hold on the Jewish people, for it is that which is closest to the inner life. In their ghettoes, where they have been cut off from a free life and the inspiration of Nature, they have yet given birth to some of the world's greatest musicians during the last two centuries. Amid happier surroundings they will develop a still greater artistic excellence. When they are a peasant people, as well as a town people, they may achieve that supreme creative genius in music which has been lacking in their famous composers of the nineteenth century. Such a genius can come only from the Folk. The reproach that Jews are imitative in art will pass away in a free Jewish environment, where Jewish artists can express the life and thought of the Jewish people.

Another Art school of the new Palestine population which has attracted general notice, is the " Bezalel " of Jerusalem, named after the craftsman who designed the Tabernacle of the Israelities in the wilderness. It is a practical Arts and Crafts institute as well as a school, and has as its two objects to revive among the Palestine community the skill in the applied arts for which the Jews were distinguished in the Dark or Middle Ages, and at the same time to provide the younger generation with a useful vocation. In the ghettoes the Jewish hand lost its cunning, and the Jewish eye its sense of beauty. In the new life that is budding, that cunning, and that sense, are being recovered. The fine arts also are taught at the Bezalel, and Professor Schatz, the director, is a distinguished sculptor. But, as befits a young community, the application of beauty to the useful is more regarded than the creation of beautiful things for their own sake, and the equipment of some hundreds of young men and women with a practical skill is considered more important than the training of a number of artists. The particular branches of craft which are practised are, carpet-weaving, wood-carving, jewellery, filigree and inlaid metal work, and lace making, and before the war the artistic productions of the school were displacing rapidly, in Jerusalem, the meretricious and tawdry souvenirs of hallowed memory. The Bezalel had, too, an export trade which was growing up by leaps and bounds, and amounted in 1912 to a value of over £10,000. Exhibitions of Bezalel handiwork had been held at many of the chief centres of Europe and America, and had not only secured a large support for the school, but stirred a new pride in thousands of Jews whose respect for the people in the Holy

RENAISSANCE IN THE SCHOOLS

Cities had been weakened by mere almsgiving. The idea of the Jerusalem Jew as a bad beggar was beginning to be displaced by the idea of him as a good craftsman. As at the Jaffa Gymnasium, young men and women study and work together, and representatives of all the communities which make the microcosm of Jewry in Jerusalem are gathered in the school, where the inherited skill in certain forms of craft which is possessed by sections of the population—such as by the Yemenites in filigree, and of the Persian girls in weaving —have been turned to account. As the agricultural colonies are the pledge of the repopulation of Palestine's waste places by young Jewry, so the Bezalel is the pledge of the regeneration of the town-dwellers of Palestine by honest industry.

The war has inevitably given a set-back to the development of the Bezalel; it has not however, so far as is known, caused the closing of the Secondary Schools and Training Colleges which were started by the Hebrew enthusiasts when the struggle with the Hilfsverein broke out. To the Jews the school is the last sanctuary, and even when the nourishment of the body is wanting, he will not give up, unless violently compelled, the nurture of the mind. To-day the schools of Palestine are saving the Jewish settlement from destruction and despair, and keeping alive till happier days the spirit of the Renaissance.

The enthusiasm of the Palestinian Jews for their Hebrew culture rose, even during the war, superior to its trials. After the outbreak of hostilities between the Allies and Turkey, some 10,000 Jews of European nationality, preferring exile to forced Ottomanisation and the tender mercies of Ottoman military rule, went down to Egypt for refuge. Among them were three thousand children of school age; and as soon as it was clear that they would have to sojourn at Alexandria some time, the first care of the Refugees' committee was to provide schooling for them. The head mistress of the Evelina School at Jerusalem was among the deported, and she undertook the management of two schools in the refugee encampments which were administered by the Egyptian Government authorities. The children in their exile acquired a delightful facility alike in the language of their mother country and in the language of their protectors. Their hearts were still firmly set on the return to Palestine; they sang the songs of Zion, and talked the language of Zion, by the waters of the Nile. The Palestinian exiles contrived also to imbue with their spirit the older Jewish schools of the land of Egypt. A number of the expelled teachers found employment there; and, bringing an invincible enthusiasm to their work, secured the acceptance of Hebrew as a living language. The ravages of war may have destroyed the buildings of the Palestine Jewish schools, but they could not quell the spirit that filled those buildings, and they actually gave it greater expansion.

The war, however, has retarded for a time the creation of the crown of the educational system. The chief practical achievement of the Zionist Congress held in 1913 was to determine on the foundation of a National University in Jerusalem, and to appoint a Commission to elaborate a scheme or working project. Before the outbreak of hostilities things had got as far as the subscription of large sums for the building, and the Commission had secured the option of a worthy site. The building of the university may be delayed, but it will surely be one of the first ambitions of the Jewish people after the war to set up in Jerusalem a home of learning, which shall be the hearth of Jewish scholarship—the message of Jewish thought for the Diaspora of to-day, as the Temple was to the Diaspora of olden time. The Jew, it has been said, is born educated; and, certainly, education and appreciation of intellectual excellence is more widely spread among the masses of Jewry than among those of any other people. Education has for two thousand years been their chief weapon of defence, and the University will be the Palestine "Dreadnought."

It is notable that the great Moslem University, El Azhar, which survives to-day in Cairo, owes its design to one who was born a Jew—Jacob Ibn Killin—a convert to Islam, who as Vizier to the Fatimite Caliph, transformed El Azhar from mosque to university. But the Jewish University of Jerusalem will not be like El Azhar, a stronghold of mediævalism and inflexible theology, but a home of modern and progressive thought. For it will owe its existence in the first place to the aspirations of the young Palestinians for more knowledge. Some two hundred of them were before the war attending the college of the American Mission of the Jesuit Fathers in Beirut, which was the most important educational institution of Syria providing a professional training. That the Jewish students were not much affected by the underlying spirit of the college is proved by the fact that they had a flourishing Zionist society and a club of their own; yet it is a pity that they should have to seek their higher education and spend the impressionable years of adolescence in a strange atmosphere. A Hebrew university at Jerusalem would draw its students, however, not only from Palestine, but from the whole of the Diaspora. It would be to Jewry what Oxford and Cambridge are to the whole of the British Empire; and more than that. Hitherto hundreds of Russian and Polish Jews, denied higher education in their own land, have flocked to the universities of France, Switzerland, and Germany. In the future they will eagerly turn to Palestine and receive their enlightenment in Jewish surroundings, and in their own national tongue. Much of the ardent thought which now runs to waste, because nourished in an alien and semi-hostile environment, will be fruitful when it develops according to its special bent and in tranquillity—inspired, too, by a national spirit.

The University of Jerusalem will be not only a symbol of the spiritual hegemony of Palestine over the whole of Jewry, but it will be the actual radiating centre of the Jewish Renaissance. The scholars, the poets, and the philosophers of the dispersed communities will gather there, and in the fulness of time it will be the seat of a revived Sanhedrin which will develop, in accordance with the thought of the day, the heritage of Jewish Law. There will be established the embodiment of the catholic conscience of Judaism which alone can sanction, and secure general acceptance for, a reform of the religious practice. Jewry has been without an authoritative body of the kind for a thousand years, since the line of the Gaonim came to an end; and its progressive development has, in consequence, been arrested. With the re-establishment of the true centre, Judaism will again be able to develop freely. However, it is the university, and not the Synod, which will be the moulding force of the religious, as well as of the national, culture. Religion indeed cannot be separated from the rest of culture in Judaism. And if the elementary, and secondary, and technical schools will be primarily for the part of the Jewish people living in Palestine, the University of Jerusalem will be for the whole congregation of Israel. "From Zion shall go forth the Law."

Very early in the history of the Zionist movement it was declared by Herzl that there was no remedy for the Jewish troubles except the return to Judaism: "Zionism is the return to Jewry before the return to the Jewish land." That there should be in Palestine a dissociation of Jewish national life from religion would be an unthinkable solution. The great need of the East to-day is to revive the religious influence and inspiration required to strengthen the old faiths, which have been rudely shaken by the rapid incursion of Western rationalism. The East is absorbing European science, it is not receptive of European social ethics; and in the younger generation, educated according to Western ideas, cynical self-interest becomes the dominant motive of conduct. The Jewish people, with their deep religious sense and their wonderful religious tradition, should play a great part in regenerating the people of the Eastern world upon a fresh basis of morality—" a pure religion breathing household laws "—and anything which impairs the hold of Judaism is a loss to humanity.

Wells has presaged a religious revival as one of the deeper effects of the war. Mankind, after the ordeal by fire, he thinks, will acknowledge the kingship of God in the way the children of Israel were called on to acknowledge it after the Babylonian captivity. National patriotism and pride of race will be subordinated to the sense that all men are subject to one Universal Ruler, and are members of one human society. What people has such capacity to give reality to this idea as that whose prophets taught it 2,500 years ago, when the military powers of the world had shattered their strength against one another, and the doctrine of " blood and iron " had been exploded by the fall of Babylon? Viewed in the light of the world movements impelled by the war, the question of religious education in the schools of Palestine is not a matter of local or parochial interest only, but is integrally bound up with the significance of the Return of the Jews to the Land. Its solution is one of the chief problems which will confront the new régime.

CHAPTER VIII

THE WAR AND THE SETTLEMENTS

THE Jewish population of Palestine suffered considerably between the years 1911 and 1913 from the Tripolitan and Balkan Wars. The development of agriculture and industry, as well as of commerce and of communications, which had been rapidly proceeding in the previous decade, was gravely handicapped; and the Ottoman Government pressed its demands for taxes and military service with greater strictness than heretofore. Under the Ottoman law all adult males of Ottoman nationality were liable to be called up for three years' service, but a man unwilling to serve could redeem the obligation by payment of thirty pounds Turkish (£28). Many of the Jewish colonists, and more of the town-dwellers, retained their foreign nationality of origin after settling in Palestine, principally with a view to escaping this Turkish military conscription—which is not served under easy conditions. Of the rest, many redeemed themselves and enriched the Turkish exchequer; but still a considerable number were taken off to the army.

When the Balkan War at length came to an end, there was a great stirring in the country. Projects of reforms, which had been delayed by the years of hostilities and unrest, were revived, and the representatives of syndicates for opening up new areas, making new railways, and constructing new ports, arrived and set to work. There was a promise of something in the nature of a Palestine boom. The French Government, as it was publicly announced, obtained a concession for a railway from Rayak in Syria, between Damascus and Beirut, to Jerusalem, to run parallel for half its course with the Hedjaz railway, and afterwards to pass through the centre of the country till it met the existing French-owned line from Jaffa to Jerusalem at Ramleh. A group of French capitalists, moreover, were granted a concession for building ports at Jaffa and Haifa, of which men had talked and consuls had written for years and years. A Belgian syndicate was to develop the mineral wealth of the Dead Sea region, and one of the big oil trusts was to tap new reservoirs of petrol in the Jordan valley, and the Hauran beyond. Jewish hopes of agricultural expansion and industrial development likewise ran high. In the spring of 1914, a remarkable number of representative men visited the country, and after the U.S. Ambassador Morgenthau's journey, it was announced that a Commission would be sent out in the autumn from America to report on what should be done for the general welfare of the inhabitants. I spent a few weeks in the Jewish settlements early in the summer of 1914, and shared in the general conviction that a bright era of progress was opening. The atmosphere in the colonies was full of plans for the purchase of land to increase the Jewish agricultural colonisation and lay out fresh garden suburbs; and the American Zionist Societies in particular were beginning to take a leading part in the labour of expansion and to bring a fresh store of enterprise and initiative to the work.

When the tempest of war suddenly burst upon the world in August, 1914, it left Palestine, at first, comparatively unshaken. At the time it was not expected that the Ottoman Empire would join in the fray, and the chief consequence of the outbreak of hostilities was here, as in other neutral countries, a financial crisis. The gold and silver currency, always scarce in the country, was almost entirely stopped, the paper money issued by the Government was of doubtful value, and the colonists devised a system of credit among themselves. They issued promises to pay, which, characteristically, were in Hebrew; and these scraps of paper passed as coin of the realm. The colonists trusted the credit of the few men of means among them, and they were prepared to risk the loss in the case of a note emanating from one of their own number.

Their communistic sense was strengthened in them, and they formed societies for relieving the distress of any who could not stand the shock of the world-quake. A great rôle was also played by certified cheques of the Anglo-Palestine Co. (a creation of the Jewish Colonial Trust, " the financial instrument of Zionism "), which had become the universal bank for the Jewish settlers, and served also a large part of the Arab population.

In the towns, where the stringency was greater and the population less self-supporting, a remarkable organisation of mutual help was built up, and the fabric of educational institutions, so recently erected, was kept intact despite the difficulties of the crisis. After a month or two of indecision, the war began to come closer and make greater inroads on the life of all the people. Preparing for their entry into the conflict, which was already decided on, the Turks pressed men for military service more relentlessly than ever, and made requisitions of provisions and transport for the army. The Jewish colonists had to give up their horses and carts, to open their stores of grain, to cut down their trees, to hand up their arms, to receive the soldiers billeted on them, and to provide parties for defensive works. A little later came the declaration of war between the Ottoman Empire and the Powers of the Entente. Djemal Pasha, one of the leaders of the Young Turk party, who had proved himself brave in the Balkan War and active thereafter and had become Minister of Marine, was sent as Generalissimo of the Army of Syria. And plans were laid for a Turkish invasion of Egypt.

This was of bad omen for the Jewish settlements, for Palestine, and especially the coast plain of Judæa, was the natural basis for such a campaign. The Turkish headquarters was in fact fixed at Beersheba. In the world war one of the world's historical battlefields was again to know the tramp of armies. The struggle of nations has invoked everywhere the negation of the doctrine of Rousseau that war is a relation of States, and not of peoples. In every belligerent country the individual, sooner or later, has been identified with his State, and the mitigation introduced into the practice of war during the nineteenth century of allowing peaceful enemy aliens to reside in the belligerent country, so long as they were of good behaviour, was rudely swept away. Some thousands of the Jewish settlers in Palestine had preserved their foreign nationality, or at least had not assumed Ottoman citizenship, and upon the declaration of war they were given the alternative of accepting forthwith that citizenship and its obligations, or of leaving the country at short notice. Many chose the former course, especially among those who had a stake in the land. Becoming naturalised Ottomans they remained on their farms. They were promised release from military service, and were prepared to take the risk of the Turks keeping faith. Some thousands, however, of Russian, French, and English subjects, preferred a fresh exile to the tender mercies of the Ottoman Government and the prospect of famine which was already looming. They were mainly sprung from the towns, and a considerable proportion were recipients of the Chaluka; but some hundreds were labourers (Poalim) of the colonies who were willing to take their part in the war, but desired to serve in the ranks of the Allies. These were afterwards embodied in the Zion Mule Corps which went through the Gallipoli campaign from beginning to end, as a transport unit of the British army at Cape Hellas, and acquitted itself well under the command of Colonel Paterson, who published a very popular book on the achievements of his little Jewish force.

Few of the thousands who desired to leave the country had the means to get away on the very limited number of neutral vessels that were still calling at the Palestinian or Syrian ports. But the American Government, represented at Constantinople by Mr. Morgenthau, who had developed a deeply sympathetic interest in Palestine during that very summer, came to the rescue. The United States cruisers, *Tennessee* and *Des Moines* and *Chester*, which were in Mediterranean waters, arrived off Jaffa and Beyrout, and in turn carried off thousands of refugees. The land of Egypt once again, as in the days of the Bible, was to be the land of refuge. Together with the exiled monks and nuns and the European Christians, the thousands of Jewish alien enemies of the Turks, were brought away with such only of their possessions as they could carry with them, and landed at Alexandria. They were not all compulsory exiles; some subjects of Spain and other neutral countries came away with the stream, anticipating—not, as was proved by events, without reason—evils to come. The American cruisers deposited their living freights at Port Said and Alexandria, and there they were generously assisted by the British authorities, who formed regular refugee camps. They settled down to make what they hoped would be a short sojourn—a sojourn, however, which now, three years later, is still not ended. During this period of exile the greater number have achieved independence. Some 3,000 still remain in the Government camps, for the most part women, children, and old men. They have lived under hard conditions, but their presence in Egypt has had a reviving effect on the local Jewry, which had for long been sunk in a lethargy and indifferent to the national ideal. At first the refugees had with them in their new surroundings few of their home leaders; most of the men and women

WAR AND THE SETTLEMENTS 185

of influence and personality had chosen to stand by their Palestine work. But in the beginning of the year 1916, the Turks, pursuing a more aggressive policy, turned against the heads of the Jewish institutions in Palestine who were of enemy origin. Exile, either within or without the Ottoman Empire, was the choice they offered, and many more made their way to Egypt.

Djemal Pasha, the local autocrat, issued an almost savage proclamation against all Zionist enterprises, threatening with extreme penalties any who should make outward profession of adherence to the Jewish nationalist cause, or show the Jewish flag. He disarmed the Jewish police of the colonies, the *Shomerim*, who were the only security against robbery. And, what was even more serious, he took extreme measures against the principal Jewish financial institution, the Anglo-Palestine Bank, which had become the mainstay of the colonies. The bank was constituted as an English trading company, and therefore came within the scope of the action taken against enemy concerns. It was suddenly ordered to liquidate its business in Palestine, and to shut down all its branches. The distress of the masses, owing to want of money and of food, increased day by day. The Turkish army destined for the invasion of Egypt scoured the country-side for provisions and made pitiless requisitions. It cut down the trees and laid bare the forest colony of Chederah. Again it was American Jewry which came to the aid of its hard-pressed brethren. It had the means, and it gave them, as its way is when moved, with a large hand. Soup kitchens were organised for feeding those in greatest want, and some thousands more of the destitute were brought away to Egypt, and admitted to the refugee camp at Alexandria.

The Palestine settlement, however, had to undergo other trials. On top of the Turkish requisitions, which denuded the country-side, a plague of locusts of unparalleled severity burst on the devoted land in the spring of 1915. It passed at the same time over Egypt, but there the whole manhood was called out, and marshalled on scientific lines by the central and local administration, to combat the pest, and the danger was kept within bounds. In Palestine no scheme of fighting the insects existed, and the administration was unequal to the task of improvising an adequate defence. It made a spasmodic effort, and called in the help of the Jewish agronomist Aaron Aaronson, who was director of the Agricultural Experimental Station. He, indeed, organised the population of the Jewish colonies, but he could not, with the insufficient means at his disposal, organise the undisciplined and ignorant and scattered Arab population. The orchards and plantations and vineyards fell a helpless prey to the swarms of insects, and the work of a generation was destroyed in a month. Owing to the dearth of food, various diseases ravaged the people; and owing to the lack of drugs and medicine the death rate among the sick was terribly high; typhus, small-pox, typhoid, and cholera followed each other. Though out of the immediate war zone, the country was suffering the worst horrors of war.

Still the people never lost their zeal for the spiritual goods of the Yishub. Neither war nor want could undermine their love of education, and their ardour for their precious Hebraism. The schools all continued in session; and this at least may be said for the Turkish authorities, they did not for a time attempt to close them. Where institutions were staffed by enemy subjects, as with the schools of the French Alliance Israélite and the Evelina de Rothschild girls' school, the enemy teachers had indeed to leave the country. But the authorities permitted substitutes to be appointed from among the Ottoman-Jewish subjects, and the only innovation in the curriculum was to substitute Turkish for the enemy language. The two directors of the Gymnasium at Jaffa, who were Russian subjects by origin, were both compelled to go, despite the Ottomanisation of the institute. But, even so, the school kept its doors open, and the directors carried on a vigorous propaganda for their Hebraic method in the countries of their exile. One of them led the movement for the foundation of a Hebrew high school in Alexandria for the elder children of the refugees, and the other went as an apostle of Hebraism to America.

A new phase of Palestine's trials opened in 1917 when the British army, which had crossed the wilderness of Sinai, passed the frontiers. England came as a deliverer of the Arab and Jewish peoples from the neglect and misgovernment of the Turks; and the Turks, conscious that the invader would be welcomed, wreaked their spite on the defenceless Jewish settlers. In accordance with the merciless policy initiated elsewhere by their allies, they moved the civil population away as the hostile armies approached. The inhabitants of Gaza, who comprised only a few hundred Jews, and the Jewish inhabitants of Jaffa, who numbered some fifteen thousand —but not the more numerous Moslems—were forced to leave their homes when the British forces, in the spring of 1917, reached the Wadi Ghuzzeh. The deportation at Jaffa was attended with every hardship and some circumstances of wanton cruelty. The exiles had no city of refuge to which to turn. Egypt was now closed to them, and the humanising mediation of the United States could no longer be exercised. They had therefore to throw themselves on the charity of their brethren higher up the country in various settlements who were already desperately hard pressed; and the general distress was increased. Very little news leaked through neutral countries of what was happening, but the tidings that came were increasingly alarming. A list of the relative prices of the chief commodities before the war and at the beginning of the fourth year of the struggles, which was published in *Palestine*, September 8th, 1917, speaks for itself:

	Price in 1914 Francs	Price in 1917 Francs
Bread per rotl (=about 5½ lbs.)	1	11
Sesame	2	27
Coal	0·25	1·90
Petroleum	1	30
Salt	0·25	4
Lentils	0·90	13·50
Tea	3	22·5
Wood	7·50	40

In Jerusalem, particularly, where the Turks fixed the headquarters of their Palestine army, the situation of the Jews, who always lived in congested areas and on the margin of destitution, recalled the horrors of the great siege which was the death agony of the nation.

"The misery of the poor," wrote a correspondent from Jerusalem, at the end of June, "is unspeakable. The roads are lined with starving persons who lie about begging for a mouthful of bread. The poor Jews sell all their belongings and clothes, linen and bed covers, to the soldiers to get a few metalliks for food." The words of the writer of Lamentations were realised: "The young children ask bread, and no man breaketh it unto them."

Among the lands martyred by the war, Palestine has a principal place. The Belgium of the East, as it has been called, its people have suffered like the Belgians of the West; yet throughout the times of stress and suffering the Jews have held fast to their infant culture, and never lost their ancient hope. These 100,000 sufferers are the pledge of the Zionist movement, for it is their presence in the Holy Land which, more than all the speeches and assemblies in the Diaspora, more than the world's Press suddenly grown universally sympathetic, focus the attention of the civilised world on the Jewish claim to the country They are therefore in a very real sense the advance guard of Jewry. Like the steadfast remnant that remained behind with Gedaliah when those of the second Captivity were taken away to Babylon, they to-day are the earnest of the Return.

The colonies will inevitably be weakened by these years of privation, and the town population will be sorely reduced, both in number and in circumstances, but the character of the people will be the stronger for having passed through the ordeal, and the title of the nationality will be strengthened by the achievement and endurance of its representatives.

One compensation of the war, too, has already been revealed. The British army, since it crossed the border, has proved the possibilities of a greater prosperity which will speedily make up for the destruction wrought by the Turkish army of occupation. In the least favoured part of the country it has found, and developed, water for hundreds of thousands of men and hundreds of thousands of animals, where before a few hundred Bedouins half tilled the fields and pastured their animals. Where there is water in the East there is a way to fruitfulness, and it needs only the will to bring fruition.

As too the army of deliverance proceeds it will in simple truth extend the boundaries of justice and good government, and it will open up a new era in the annals of the Bible Land.

It is no wonder that many in these days of miracles have come to believe again in the literal fulfilment of prophecy. For they have seen before their eyes a highway built from Egypt into Syria, and the thirsty land becoming a spring of waters, and the wilderness a pool. The days of war have brought the beginning of fulfilment, and the days of peace will surely continue it to the full realisation of the dreams and hopes of the seers of 2,500 years ago, which have remained the dreams and hopes of their people.

CHAPTER IX

THE FUTURE OF THE LAND AND THE PEOPLE

THE future of Palestine, and the future of the Jewish people, have become two of the larger questions which will be treated at the Settlement of the Nations after the war. In the world struggle, of which one of the great moral issues is the right of nationalities to self-development, it is impossible to disregard the claim of the oldest surviving nationality, the veteran of history, to resume its national life. And in the redemption of the Ottoman Empire from neglect and misrule, it is impossible to disregard the claims of the people who, for a thousand years, made Palestine one of the centres of the world's civilisation, and who, during the last thirty years, have laid anew the foundations of the country's fruitfulness.

Before the war Zionism was stated, by one of its chief critics, Mr. Lucien Wolf, to be " the greatest popular movement that Jewish history has ever known." To-day it has not only multiplied manifold its adherents among the Jews, but it has been adopted by the representatives of the democracies of England, France, Russia, and the United States as the just solution of the Jewish problem. The conscience of mankind is stirred, at last, to do justice to the people which for nigh two thousand years has been a martyr for its faith ; to give, in Zangwill's words, " the Land without a People, to the People without a Land." Considerable difference of opinion, indeed, exists as to the form of political sovereignty which Palestine should receive after the war. One school favours the constitution of the country as a British colony in which the Jews will enjoy from the first a large measure of autonomy, and eventually be a self-governing nation, like the people of the Australian Commonwealth, or the Dominion of Canada. Another school favours an international régime, such as existed before the war for the management of the Danube Navigation. A third party suggests an Anglo-French condominium over all Syria. A fourth, and bolder, view, asks for the foundation, immediately, of a Jewish State or Republic, guaranteed by the League of Nations.

It is not the time now to consider the relative merits of these proposals. What is common to them all is the principle that the Jewish people shall have special rights in Palestine—not simply freedom of immigration and settlement, which have been denied to them under the Ottoman Government, but rights of self-government and powers of developing the country's resources without let or hindrance. Whatever the form of the state, Palestine is to be the National Home of the Jewish people. State sovereignty is not essential to the Jewish national ideal. Freedom for the Jew to develop according to his own tradition, in his own environment, is the main, if not the whole, demand.

It is a spiritual promise which the new Palestine pre-eminently holds out for mankind; but yet the material prospects of the country are worthy of consideration. As the meeting-place of two continents it has to-day, as it had throughout antiquity, a singular political and geographical importance. Its position, to the east of the Suez Canal, the great interoceanic waterway, serves but to increase that peculiar importance. The railway has taken the place of the road as the means of communication between countries, but it follows the lines of the road. And it is along the vale of Esdraelon—from Haifa eastward to the Jordan—and thence to Damascus, and along the Maritime plain —from Haifa southward to the river of Egypt (El-Arish)—and thence to the Nile delta, where thousands of years ago the armies and caravans of Asia met the armies and caravans of Africa, that to-morrow the railroad linking India to Egypt must pass. Here men seeking to regenerate the Land of Promise will find the overland route to India and China as of old, in looking for the seaways to the Indies, they found America. The military line built between 1916 and 1917 by the British army from the Suez Canal to Gaza has since been connected with the military railway built by the Turkish army in the same period from Jerusalem to Beersheba, and thus, through the exigencies of the war, the highway from Egypt into Syria has been made.

Palestine had already before the war a considerable network of railways. The oldest lines are those between Jaffa and Jerusalem and between Damascus and El Mezeirib in the Hauran, both owned by French companies, the first mainly designed for the tourist traffic, the second for the transport of corn. Of much greater length and importance is the Hedjaz line linking Syria and Arabia, which was built by the Turkish Government —primarily for the pilgrims of Mecca—and opened some eight years ago as far as Medina. Running from Damascus southward through the Hauran and the eastern provinces of Palestine, Gilead and Moab, to Arabia Petræa and Arabia Felix, it opens up to economic and commercial enterprise a vast district, once one of the world's granaries and—as its ruins show—populous and prosperous, but for centuries abandoned to the marauding Bedouin. A branch of the Hedjaz line from Deria in the Hauran to Haifa connects it with the sea, and another small extension of that branch to Acre encircles the bay that forms Palestine's natural harbour. Damascus, too, is now connected with Aleppo by a French line passing through Homs and Hama, and the Bagdad railway, which was designed to run from the coast of Asia Minor to the shores of the Persian Gulf and to be connected with Aleppo, has been nearly completed during the war.

Thus the linking up of the Near East and the Far East, and of Europe and the whole Orient is well on the way to achievement. Haifa will be one of the principal *débouchés* of this trunk system; and when European enterprise is unhampered, its bay, bounded by the length of Carmel on the south and the promontory of Acre on the north, will be again a haven for great ships, as it was in the days when Solomon was building the Temple, or the Franks fought the Saracens for the glory of God.

Since the beginning of the war too, the Turkish Government has completed the chain connecting Haifa with Jerusalem by a line branching off from Afuleh, a village hard by the ancient Megiddo (the Armageddon of the Bible), and passing through Samaria and Nablous into Judæa. With the forging of the last link in this railway system, through Beersheba to Gaza, Palestine has become the nodal point, not of two, but of three continents. The construction of these railways in Palestine increases, of course, the economic possibilities of the country. The interior of the country will henceforth be linked up, not only with the ports of Syria, but with the important markets of Egypt. Just as Lord Kitchener twenty-three years ago, by his military railway across the Nilian sands, prepared the way for a peaceful reclamation of the Sudan from neglect, so the British army, by the railway flung across the sands of Sinai, has prepared the way for the restoration of Palestine to its old productiveness.

Agriculture has remained from Biblical times the chief pursuit of the inhabitants, and for some time the economic development must be largely agricultural. The experience of the Jewish settlements has proved that the ancient fertility of the country may be completely restored by an industrious and intelligent population. The soil indeed is more like to that of California than of any other part of the globe; and the application of modern science to its resources will quickly undo the waste of centuries. All the authorities agree that the ground is good; it is a question only of irrigation. An immense water power, which, in the East especially, is the key of prosperity, is at present allowed to run to waste. Almost all the stream of the Jordan, which should be to Palestine what the Nile is to Egypt, flows useless into the Dead

FUTURE OF LAND AND PEOPLE 199

Sea to be evaporated. The systematic damming of the river would be a simple undertaking. From Tiberias to the Dead Sea there is a fall of ten feet a mile, and it is estimated that in that stretch of eighty miles, fifty dams could be erected for the irrigation scheme. From each such lake water would be drained out, with high-level canals contouring the hills, and giving perennial irrigation to the hothouse of the Jordan valley, which would become the greatest productive district in the world. So, too, the other streams and watercourses of the country will be dammed, and new areas will be won for intensive cultivation.

A beginning has been made with the irrigation of the orchards around Jaffa, from the Nahr-el-Auja, which has a full and deep stream all the year round; but the River Kedron, flowing through Esdraelon, and all the many streams which are full in winter and are dry beds in the summer, are completely unharnessed. They may readily be turned into a chain of ponds and lakes and sources of abundant fruitfulness, so that the whole of the coastal plain will be a continuous stretch of gardens, cornfields, and vineyards.

The water power of Palestine's rivers will be used, too, for supplying electricity, as well for industrial as for agricultural purposes. While in its southern course from Tiberias the fall of the Jordan is gradual, in its upper course its falls are much more sudden. In its first twenty-five miles it drops nearly two thousand feet, or about seventy feet a mile. The Yarmuk, one of its chief tributaries, rolls headlong from the Hauran plateau to its junction, with a total fall of over 1,000 feet. Were the falls of these two rivers utilised, it is estimated that sufficient energy could be created to supply Acre, Haifa, and Tyre and the intervening country, i.e. the whole of the rich plain of Esdraelon and its sea-board, with electricity for lighting and power. There are other rivers in this land of mountain ranges and valleys which have an almost equal fall, more particularly those which descend from the plateau east of the Jordan into the main waterway. The use of all this potential electric energy will be a factor of greater consequence for the restoration of Palestine than the introduction of Western machinery, which has already been initiated by the Jewish settlers with striking results. It will not only revolutionise agriculture by rendering feasible large schemes of irrigation, but it will be the foundation of the growth of important industries.

Palestine has already a considerable industrial population among the Jewish town-dwellers, who have hitherto been only half employed. After the war, when Jewish immigration on a big scale is organised, it will have a much larger labour force of the kind. Hitherto, the only considerable manufactures have been

FUTURE OF LAND AND PEOPLE

of soap from the olive berry, and of souvenirs from the olive wood. But mineral deposits are known to exist which, already before the war, promised industrial expansion. Phosphates have been mined in the region of Gilead, and the Dead Sea is an untapped reservoir of chemical wealth. The Biblical description of Canaan as a land "whose stones are iron, and out of whose hills thou mayest dig brass," may be justified when men start to survey, not only, as in the past, for the monuments of an old civilisation, but also for minerals to which the industry of a new population may be applied.

The Jews have given to Europe great names in the history of chemical research; and among those who go out to Palestine will certainly be men who will know how to utilise for the development of their country the forces and resources with which Nature has endowed it. Oil, too, has been struck in the land east of Jordan, and it is said that the arid country of the Negeb, the Southern wilderness, on the surface so inhospitable, contains veins of coal. But even if these hopes are disappointed, the harnessing of the electric energy which is stored up in the rivers and falls would provide the motive force for all the machinery required for the utilisation of the products of a redeemed Palestine, once an industrious population is settled in the land. The cotton of the Jordan valley may equal the cotton of the Nile valley when irrigation has reclaimed those wasted fields, and, when looms have been set up, part of the cotton of Egypt, too, may more profitably be spun in Palestine than in Lancashire. The Orient sends the greater part of its natural wealth to the West to-day to be worked up because it lacks just that class of enterprising and diligent working people which the Jewish resettlement will bring to Palestine.

Nevertheless, although there is room for a considerable industrial development and for commercial enterprise, and the trend of events before the war gave promise of those things, yet for some time the chief expansion must be agricultural. The Jews have in the first place to make the soil theirs, to fill the land and develop it. " Be fruitful, and multiply," may well be their motto. The population had considerably increased during the half-century before the war by reason of Jewish immigration, but Palestine is still in great measure an empty land. It will be emptier after the ravages of the war. In 1914 the country had some 700,000 inhabitants, but, outside the towns, only about 250,000 Arabs were living on the land, and but eight per cent of the soil was cultivated.

Historical Palestine—the territory between Dan on the north and Beersheba on the south, and between the Syrian desert on the east and the sea on the west—is about the same

FUTURE OF LAND AND PEOPLE

size as Wales. It has been called "the least of all lands"; and, for the home of one of the historic nations, it seems small. You can see its whole length and breadth from the summit of several of the mountains, and there is no country which is spread so clearly, as on a map, before the traveller. And yet it embraces some 10,000 square miles, 6,000 to the west of the Jordan and 4,000 to the east.

The late Colonel Conder, R.E., who spent years in surveying and exploring its ruins, calculated, from the records of the past, that at one time it supported at least ten millions of people, and, from the natural features, that it could immediately maintain three or four times the existing number of inhabitants. The density of population is now only seventy, and, excluding the towns, less than half that number, per square mile. Even without the foundation of industries, by the good organisation of agriculture, and by the terracing and afforesting of the hill country, that population might be trebled and quadrupled. During the last century the population of Egypt has increased fourfold, while the country has remained almost wholly agricultural. The rabbis of old compared Palestine to a deer whose skin grows when it is well fed. The hills of Judæa and Samaria and Galilee, that are to-day covered with ruins, will be covered with hamlets when they are well nourished.

Nor need the Palestine of the future be

confined to its historic borders; Jewish colonisation may extend to the whole territory which was contained in the Promise. From the Mediterranean to the Euphrates, and from Lebanon to the river of Egypt—this is the territory which was given to the chosen people. All this area, this Greater Palestine, cries for a population to redeem it from the neglect and decay of centuries, and all of it is full of historical associations for the Jews. The plateaus of Gilead and Moab, and the plains that stretch away to the Tigris and the Euphrates, may be reclaimed by Jewish enterprise and industry, no less than the hills of Judæa and Samaria, and the green slopes of Galilee. Two years before the war a group of Russian Zionists had actually acquired land in the neighbourhood of Rafa, on the edge of the desert over the Egyptian border, for settlement. And the green oasis of Khan-Yunis with its orchards, rising like a little Damascus out of the rolling plains of Philistia, has brought it home to thousands of the British army that the Holy Land may still be made to flow with milk and honey even to its extreme limits.

The congested Jewish town population of Palestine will be reduced, after the war, partly by diversion to the land, partly by the creation of industries which will immediately be required in new centres when a steady immigration begins. In Turkey's Asiatic

FUTURE OF LAND AND PEOPLE 205

dominions there are a quarter of a million Jews outside Palestine—in the capital, in Smyrna, Damascus, Aleppo, and Bagdad—and many of these urban workers may be enticed back to the land; while a further substantial contribution of the more active and enterprising, industrial and commercial, elements will certainly be made by the Jewish inhabitants of Salonica, of whom there were more than 70,000 before the war. Another formerly Turkish district, the Yemen, on the south of Arabia, possesses a reservoir of Jewish labour in the 50,000 people who at present eke out a wretched life in subjection to fanatical Arab tribes; the whole community is eager to move when its emigration can be organised. Larger sources of a sturdy population to fill the waste spaces have only awaited the call of the new Cyrus. There are the homeless millions of Poland and Lithuania, exiled during the war and little likely to find a welcome back to their old homes when the hostilities are over. For them emigration is the only solution of the conflict of nationalities, and a steady stream will flow eastward to the land of Jewish promise as well as westward to the land of material prospects.

For the Jews in Russia proper, the war indeed has brought a new hope and a wonderful redemption, but it has not destroyed or impaired the old hope, or shaken the faith in the redemption for which earlier generations have prayed. It is a shallow reading of the Russo-Jewish character which finds in the civil emancipation the knell of Zionist aspiration. For them the glowing promises of statesmen in war-time, or the glib words of delegates at a Peace Conference, will not prepare the new heaven on a new earth. For they are Zionists, not only by repulsion from their environment, but by enthusiasm for the remaking of their own people. There are, too, the thousands in the ancient settlements in Georgia and Turkestan, looking with the simple faith of old for the chance of hastening the coming of the Messiah. There are, lastly, the idealistic bodies of young Zionists in every Jewish community of the West, who see in Palestine alone the chance of realising " the good life " and the Jewish hope. Already small bands from all these scattered communities have fixed their home in Jerusalem. And, when Palestine is freely opened, the yearning for the Holy Land will be as strong as the yearning for the Holy City, and will more powerfully inspire to action. The love of the country will strengthen and revivify the love of the religion; and the spirit of the land will weld the diverse mass into a conscious nation. Even as the prophets foretold, " When the trumpet call is sounded the people will go up from the ends of the earth."

It has often been made an objection to Zionist hopes that the Moslem Arabs now in

FUTURE OF LAND AND PEOPLE 207

possession of Palestine lands, already numbering more than a quarter of a million, cannot be ejected, and that the country adjoining is the home of wandering tribes of Bedouins. But it is neither to be expected, nor is it desired, that the Jews should occupy and appropriate the whole country. There is ample room for the children of Esau and Jacob to live together in harmony in the land. The interests of the present and the future population in fact coincides, and it will be within the power of a just administration to secure a good understanding and co-operation between the two elements that are in origin akin and have common ties of race. The local Arab population shows no tendency to increase, and the Syrian overflow, which has hitherto turned principally to America, will be likely to find a greater attraction in the rich valleys of Anatolia when that province is opened up, than in the more mountainous country to the south. The revival of the national life of the Arabs will be achieved in the home of the race, and in Mesopotamia which is rich with the traditions of their glory. The Jews, only, feel Palestine to be their Fatherland, the cradle of their history and the goal of their endeavour. It is the Jews alone who will make any large and systematic immigration into Palestine; and it is Jewish enterprise and enthusiasm and devotion which will have to reclaim it to its former place.

As to the Christian population, it is to be remembered that, even before the war, there were fewer Christians than Jews—less than a hundred thousand, including the 80,000 natives of different sects. The rest were mainly members of religious orders, and there were only small groups of European Christian residents in the towns. Save for the small German settlements, which had their origin sixty years ago in a religious enthusiasm that died away, none have been attempted during the last century, and the experience of the Swedish peasants and American mystics, who sought to establish an ideal community in Jerusalem, suggests that religious enthusiasm, when divorced from national sentiment, will not be strong enough to hold to the land those who come from a different national environment. The Christian interest will remain then rather that of pilgrims than of pioneers; and it will be centred on the holy sites. The Pope has expressed his approval of the Zionist aspiration to make Palestine again a Jewish homeland, and the arrangements about the Holy Places, or about jurisdiction over the persons and property of the religious orders, will be the mere details of diplomatic arrangement, which cannot affect the main lines of development of the country.

The civilisation of Palestine can only be enriched by the presence of diverse elements. The idea of a religious test for settlement in the country is a mere fantasy. A Jewish country will be open to men of all creeds and all nationalities as fully as the Anglo-Saxon countries. In the free state, as Zunz well said, it is not the Jew who rules over the Christian, or the Christian who rules over the Jew; it is justice that rules.

Western ideas and Western methods, however, will be introduced into the villages and fields of Palestine, neither by Moslem Arabs nor by European Christians, but by Jews, who will come from Europe with the determination of building up a fresh and a full national life. For nearly a thousand years the Jews have lived predominantly in Europe, and they will return to Palestine as the upholders of European culture, not only in its material, but in its deeper intellectual and social aspects. "We mean to go to Palestine," said Max Nordau at the Hague Zionist Congress (1907), "as the standard-bearers of civilisation, with the mission of extending the moral frontiers of Europe to the Euphrates."

Palestine was a hearth of Western civilisation, from the time of Alexander the Great almost unbrokenly till the thirteenth century, when the Tartar hordes burst upon it, and laid waste its towns and villages. The grandiose ruins of Hellenistic towns on the east of the Jordan, the Roman basilicas of Jerusalem and Bethlehem, and the massive walls of Crusaders' castles up and down the country, bear witness to the succession of brilliant Western civilisations which have left their stamp on the land of the Hebrew prophets. The West, on the other hand, has here met and learned from the East. From contact with the progressive Arab culture of the day the Crusaders and merchants brought back to Europe, not only the arts and commodities of the East, but also its science and philosophy. The Jews of that period were a link between the Arabs and Christians, fulfilling a mediating function, and preparing the way for the Reformation and the Renaissance. The Jews who now return to Palestine will accomplish the converse service, bringing to their old home the ideas and the inventions of the countries of their sojourn, and preparing the way for the Reform and Revival of the East.

A tendency towards secularism has caused some misgivings to sympathisers with Zionist aspirations, who fear the growth of an aggressively materialistic national spirit. But the genius of the country will surely revive the deeper spiritual powers latent in the race, which centuries of repression have diverted but never crushed. The immigration to Palestine will be, largely, not of adventurers seeking material gain, but of those anxious to realise an ideal, and therefore it will have a heightened consciousness of the aims of corporate life. Spiritually the infant communities of the pre-war settlement marked the beginnings of a new Hebraic life. Palestine, as Herzl conceived it, was to be the Old-new-Land (*Altneuland*) in which the spiritual heritage of the past should be combined with the social dreams of the present, by the people whose history embraces the whole of civilisation. In outward and in inward things it was to excel. The villages and cities were to be better planned, the houses and homesteads more beautiful and attractive; universal education and co-operative enterprise, and other devices of the Socialist state-craft for the happiness of the mass, would be established from the beginning.

Side by side with these ideals of the modern commonwealth, Hebraic institutions making for equality—such as the Sabbatical year, the year of release and the Jubilee—would be revived, and become the basis of a happier social order than that which has grown up in Europe. The people who have given to mankind the founders of modern Socialism, when they have the opportunity to work out their political and social institutions on their own lines, will, it may be hoped, avoid the economic evils that have beset young political communities and reassert their function of spiritual teachers. A new generation of Maccabees will arise in this new Judæa who will spread the profounder aspects of European culture through the East, endowing it perhaps with that religious quality which is required to move the Orient. The Jew will be the ideal interpreter of West to East, and of East to West, for his history and his habit of mind make him kin, on the one side, to the Semitic peoples devoted to God and, on the other, to the Western masses devoted to human progress. He will be the reconciling element to bring back the Semites to community of thought and action with the rest of the civilised world, and will thus lay the foundation of a true concord of the races.

The events of the past century belied the high expectations of complete social and political emancipation for the Jews which accompanied the Vienna Congress of 1815, but they have, also, first revived and then transformed the national yearning for restoration to the old Home into a national movement. Jewish hopes will run high again at the congress—of 1919 ?—which is to inaugurate a new and stabler era of human brotherhood and international peace. But they will be centred now, not on civil emancipation but on national redemption, not on the means to individual freedom but on the goal of a people's striving. Palestine for nearly two thousand years has been the object of their aspirations. At last the dream is to be reality. And if the thought of a restored national life in Palestine has been an inspiration to a people, the realisation of that people's national life in Palestine will be an inspiration to humanity.

FUTURE OF LAND AND PEOPLE

For generations the Jew has disdained his present and kept his eyes steadily fixed on the future, " living on hope, and, on that very account, eternal, like hope." And now the day of fulfilment dawns and Jewry shall live, for a present worthy of its past, and preparing a worthy future.

"Thy sun shall no more go down; neither shall thy moon withdraw itself: for the Lord shall be thine everlasting light, and the days of thy mourning shall be ended.

. . . . . .

"A little one shall become a thousand, and a small one a strong nation; I the Lord will hasten it, in his time."

APPENDIX

THE REDEMPTION OF JUDÆA

THE REDEMPTION

Sketches on the Advance of the British Forces to Jerusalem

I. ON THE CANAL—AND BEYOND

(APRIL, 1917)

ALONG the banks of the Suez Canal and thence along the old coast road to the east you will find to-day, between the endless series of British encampments, caravans of camels passing to and fro with their burdens or lying patiently at their mangers and chewing the cud with that tranquil expression of the beast which no stress of war can disturb. There are more camels gathered here than ever were assembled in the bazaars of Cairo or Damascus. Though the defence of Egypt has been carried forward from the Canal itself to the hills and dunes of the Sinai desert and to the Land of Promise beyond, the Canal is still an integral part of the defensive scheme. Roads and railways, it is true, run out here and there eastwards from the bank, but there remains a vast hinterland unreclaimed from the desert waste in which our troops continually move. The riparian sands, if one may so call them, and the little Lancashires-in-the-desert which the loving sentiment of the North-Country Territorials has imagined, have become a network of roads and lines; and a motor-lorry will rattle you from Ballel to —— (out away in the desert) as fast as a jolting car on the roads of Connemara. But ere long you will come to a region which car or locomotive has not yet defiled, and here the camel reigns supreme. Daily he carries the food and water for the men in the extreme line of trenches and at the outposts beyond, and on his back are loaded the posts and wires which daily extend " civilisation." He bears too the material with which the line of defence is being pushed forward; he is harnessed to guns in places where motors are baffled; and he carries the ambulance of the desert, in which two men are balanced on either side of his hump.

The Camel Transport Corps, although not exactly a fighting force, has been in action and received its baptism of fire. No shell or bullet can excite the stolid, contemplative animal; but it might have been expected that the camel-drivers, fellaheen enrolled in the Egyptian villages, unarmed and untrained for war, would have run for it at the first sign of attack. Yet in fact most of them responded admirably to the call of their British officers, and stuck to their animals while bullets whizzed around. With characteristic simplicity, or it may be obstinacy, when told to bring in their camels to shelter they insisted on taking with them the blankets which are issued to every man, lest they should be stolen in their absence. Some wanted to mount a hill under fire to get their money from their tents. The contempt which a Sudanese stalwart feels for the modern long-range fighting was expressed by one headman—the more warlike Sudanese regularly act as headmen over the Egyptian fellaheen—who remarked, as the shells burst, that in his country they "fought it out with knives." But another, who possessed the little knowledge of danger which is often so dangerous, when told to leave cover and fetch his camels, declined: "Me stoppa one, Dardanelles; me no stoppa two." The camel-drivers themselves have placed a stigma on those who ran away, classing them as "Biats" (girls) who are not fit for the society of "Rigala" (men). And in some companies to-day the lines are divided between those who stayed and those who fled; and it is reward or punishment to be moved from the one to the other.

It is the paradox of modern warfare that with all the mechanical means of locomotion the progress of an army is almost always much slower than it used to be. To-day there are no brilliant dashes, and every mile of advance, even across the desert, has had to be painfully gained, and then—blessed word—"consolidated." The army which has thus, bit by bit, driven the Turk out of the desert that bounds Egypt on the east has advanced along the main track which passes near the coast-line from Africa to Asia. It is a country not of mountains and ravines but of rolling sand-dunes and green oases—Hods, as the Arabs call them—where palms, peeping out of the surrounding bareness, give that wonderful variety of colour that is characteristic of the desert. It may be likened to a sandy Switzerland in which the yellow ridges and crests take the place of snowfields and glaciers, and the clusters of date trees represent the lakes. From time immemorial it has been the domain of the Bedouins, the true gipsies, who have no home save their camels; but now it is populous with camps and bivouacs. You see before you an apparently endless vista of sandhills and palm groves, but descend the slopes a little and you will find a bustling camp gay with tents. In one hollow you will find the bonny lads from the Lowlands, in the next you will be greeted with a broad Yorkshire accent. Here the Australian and there the New Zealand flag marks the gallant rivalry of our oversea troops pushing forward their advance. Patrols of light horse scour every recess of the "Gebel," and caravans of camels, often a mile long, loaded with food and drink for man and beast, thread the ridges, from the gloaming of the dawn to the evening twilight.

ON THE CANAL—AND BEYOND

What makes life possible for the troops moving through the soft sand in the summer heat is that the sea is near, and the bathing is splendid—like the bathing at Ostend in the days before the war. A broad and level beach which would make the fortune of any resort at home stretches eastward from Port Said mile on mile. However still the day, the waves break in a continuous roll, and when the wind blows from the north the air is as fresh as on the Kentish coast; nor is there wanting, as on that coast, "a certain liveliness" from occasional bombs. But there are days when the wind is from the scorching south or the east, and then the temperature may be anything between 110 degrees and 120 degrees in the "shade"; and there is no shade. It is a fair test of endurance for the Tommies to march through the sands under this blaze, but they count it all in the day's work. Happily the desert casts out the heat by night as fast as it takes it in by day, and the evenings are always fresh.

As in the days of the Exodus, the great need of the sojourners in the desert is water. Modern engineering, with all its devices, cannot improve much on the ancient ways of finding wells in the sand. A diviner with his rod regularly accompanies the troops at each forward move, and where the rod bends in his hands the sappers dig. The modern army, however, has not a miraculous rod like that of Moses which can make the brackish water sweet. It is not difficult to find wells, but few are serviceable for the men. Camels, luckily, are not squeamish about the more or less saltiness of the water, and they will march two, or even three, days on one drink. A continual string of camels, therefore, proceeds from the bourne of civilisation, as represented by pipes and a filtered water supply, into the depths of the wilderness, loaded with trucks of fresh water for the troops beyond. Before the campaign is over the desert route from Egypt to Syria will be lined with pipes below and wires above the ground, and a railroad running between them, for the Turks have been laying these things likewise from their end. But to-day there is still a considerable interval between the two armies innocent of pipes and wires and rails; and here the camels are still the natural and necessary link.

THE REDEMPTION

II. GAZA

(MAY, 1917)

IT is amusing for us who have been in the advance from El-Arish to read in some of the picturesque chronicles of the day how the Wadi Ghuzzeh, the river of Gaza, "that just divides the Desert from the Sown," is the true geographical boundary between Egypt and Syria, marking where vegetation begins. Rafa, it appears, is but a political milestone set in the sands, and it was only at Gaza that our army entered the Land of Promise. We who have read our Bibles and who have tramped the fifty miles from the Wadi El-Arish to the Wadi Ghuzzeh know otherwise. Of old for the Children of Israel the inhospitable desert ended at the river of Egypt, the Wadi El-Arish; and for the last three months we have appreciated and enjoyed each successive stage from the barren sand to the green loveliness of the Philistine—and Turkish —stronghold. We have passed through the promise of Bourj (reminiscent of some Crusader's castle) to the fulfilment of Sheik Zoweid, and thence along rolling downs and waving meadows to Rafa, now famous not only as the scene of Sir Philip Chetwode's dashing raid, but as the site of a March race-meeting, brilliant as any gathering on Ascot's heath.

And after we passed that boundary stone at Rafa, not a sign of the desert remained, save the broad sand-dunes which fringe the sea. At our next halting-place of Khan Yunis, whence, according to tradition, Samson took Delilah to wife, we imagined ourselves in one of the home counties. Our camps lay in orchards and parks surrounded by cactus hedges, and we could pluck fruit and nuts off the trees around our bivouacs. Leaving that belt of fruitfulness, the descent to the Wadi Ghuzzeh through barley fields was almost a relapse to a commonplace greenness.

It is amusing also to read in another commentary on the first attack on Gaza that " the district through which the advance from Rafa had to be made is quite waterless; every drop of water for men and animals had to be brought up in pipes." We, and the horses and camels with us, would have been somewhat parched if we had had to depend on the pipes, but in fact there is abundant water all along the track. It only requires to be " developed "; and, though it may seem curious to the home expert, the army is provided with field companies of engineers for that purpose. Since we left El-Arish we have been put " on the country " in a new sense, and scarce a drop of water for men and animals has come by pipe. The difficulty arises only in distributing the water from the wells during the actual engagements.

Gaza at a distance looks like a smaller Damascus; a girdle of trees is spread around for two or three miles, and the town nestles amid the verdure, save the big mosque which dominates the wooded heights. To the southeast rises the natural fortress of Ali Muntar (the Watch Tower), which from time immemorial has made the town hard to capture. In former ages it must have been girt with solid walls; now it is a labyrinth of trenches and redoubts. But when the guns and snipers are at rest the vista over the gently undulating hills and the cornfields and olive groves and fruit gardens is of idyllic peace. War loses half its evil in the East because it is so free from ugliness.

Gaza, whose Hebrew name means " The Strong," has many a time caused a check in the invaders' progress. For centuries it was a centre of struggle between the Philistines and the Hebrews; and even Alexander the Great, who conquered the whole of the East in a few years, had to lay regular siege to it. A thousand years later Omar, the Arab conqueror, found it a greater stumbling-block than even Jerusalem itself; and Saladin had to make his greatest efforts before he wrested it from the Crusaders, who had established there one of the chief fortresses of the Latin kingdom. The Tartar hordes razed its walls and citadel, but Gaza remains a place of great strength and strategic importance. Here a ridge runs across the coastal plain to the Shefelah, the range of low-lying hills that front the rugged backbone of the Judæan hills; and the army that has passed it may sweep along the Valley of Sharon till it reaches Haifa and Acre, and the great plain of Esdraelon, the main artery between Egypt and Syria.

Gaza in peaceful times is the centre of a fertile agricultural district and a busy Bedouin mart. It has a population of some 35,000 souls, coming next to Jerusalem and Jaffa in the number of its inhabitants. Its trading importance is marked by the presence of some 600 Greeks and a British consular agent and a branch of the Jewish Palestine Bank, the Anglo-Palestine Company. Before the war the roadstead was visited by the smaller steamships of the Austrian-Lloyd and the Khedivieh lines for the corn traffic, although there was no regular port of call for passengers. In the way of buildings and monuments the place has not much to boast. Naturally the spot where Samson carried off the gates, and the place where he was buried, have been "identified," and there are ruins of the old citadel. The Church Missionary

Society had a school and hospital, and an enterprising German settler had erected a steam-mill (doubtless sheltering emplacements for guns). Otherwise modern ideas and methods have made little inroad, and the bazaars are hidden in narrow, tortuous lanes, characteristic of a small city and market town. They were the meeting-place of the caravans that passed between Syria and Egypt, and the Bedouins of the Sinai Peninsula had their chief markets here. Gaza was to Sinai as Damascus is to Syria.

As the first big railway station in Palestine of the trunk line from Africa to Asia, Gaza would enjoy a new importance. The fruitfulness of the country would be increased manifold when scientific methods and machinery are brought to the aid of nature, and the neglect and mischief of man are no longer allowed to frustrate the bounty of God. And among the places where civilisation will spring up anew, Gaza, which has been celebrated under the rule of Philistines and Hebrews, Persians and Hellenistic Greeks, Romans and Byzantines, Saracens and Crusaders, will surely be counted one of the new-old cities of the East.

THE REDEMPTION

III. ROSETTA, 1799-1917

(JUNE, 1917)

It is a joy to get away altogether for a little from the great city and the haunts of soldiers and the colour of khaki. The one flaw in the ease and restfulness of the convalescent homes which the bountiful organisation of the Red Cross Society has provided for the sick wounded in Egypt is that the army is " too much with us "; late and soon, getting and spending, in shops and clubs, in the street or on the sea, we constantly run into our brother officers, and must discuss the campaign or our chances of " going up the line."

The day before I was to leave Alexandria for Gaza, being now again whole, a friend proposed a trip to Rosetta. The very name sounded attractive; there is about it a breath of the old world, a suggestion of the unbroken quiet of a sleeping seaport. Rosetta has no garrison, no base camp, no convalescent home, nothing military save the ordinary posse of Egyptian coastguards. A few forts, indeed, line the bay, among them Fort Julien, in which the famous " Rosetta " stone, now in the British Museum, was discovered, giving the key to the hieroglyphic mysteries of Egypt's monuments. But the forts to-day are as ornamental as our Martello Towers.

Rosetta is some forty miles from Alexandria, beyond the bay of Aboukir, and at the mouth of one of the great branches of the Nile. The river is dammed, and the green waters of the sea flow up to the town and a good sea smell pervades the atmosphere. A fleet of fishing vessels, and the white and red sails of the Nile barges, proclaim the port. On the west a sandy spit divides Lake Edkon from the sea, but on the east the fertile fields with their crops of rice and corn witness to the boundless gifts of the Nile.

The journey to the town is interesting. We pass the villas of Alexandria's wealthy citizens and the camps where drafts from home and men returning from hospital forgather before they proceed to the front; and then we skirt the Sultan's fair demesne of Montaza, now a convalescent home. Next past Aboukir, the scene of Nelson's decisive victory over the French fleet on August 1, 1798, and the scene also of Napoleon's equally sweeping victory a year later over the Turkish army which came to drive him from Egypt. The Lord Nelson Hotel in the village still recalls our triumph, and sells tolerable beer. One other reminder of that Egyptian campaign in the last great world-war is the inundation which is known as the Lake of Aboukir. Our Expeditionary Force of the time, in order to isolate the French army, cut a passage through the dunes, and flooded the country for miles. A large part of the flooded area has been reclaimed; but some of the 150 villages which were then destroyed are still submerged.

Rosetta itself is a town of which the glory is gone, a victim to the ruthlessness of economic forces. Founded in the Middle Ages by a Caliph of Bagdad, it soon became one of the chief ports of the Eastern Mediterranean. As Alexandria lost her pride of place the bulk of Egypt's coast trade found its way through Rosetta's harbour. When Napoleon landed in Egypt, Alexandria had but 5,000 inhabitants, and Rosetta nearly twice as many. To-day Alexandria is a city of over 400,000 persons, and Rosetta stands where she was. The construction of the Mahmoudieh Canal from the Nile barrage to Alexandria has worked this change of fortune. Now Alexandria is the port of Egypt, and again one of the great commercial centres of the East. Rosetta is a local port, through which the trade of a single province passes. Its fate is like that of Galway or Westport on the west coast of Ireland, though it has not their deserted warehouses and grass-grown quays to attest what it once was. But the ruins of the houses and the sleepy Customhouse tell their tale. Red and black bricks and solid beams of wood are the architectural features of Rosetta, and the narrow and sinuous streets still show some fine dwellings. Of the mediæval walls little trace is left, but Napoleon's Gate is still pointed out. In that wonderful year of his Egyptian and Syrian campaigns Napoleon left his mark here, as on the whole Delta.

To-day the life of the place goes on scarcely ruffled by the war or by the century of progress which has passed over Egypt since the first touch of European influence was brought to the country. Aeroplanes fly over from flying schools at Aboukir, but the natives are now as used to them as to camels. It is interesting to read the report on Rosetta which was made for Napoleon by M. Jollion, "Ingénieur en Chef des Ponts et Chaussées"; it is to be found in one of the 24 volumes that contain the researches of the savants with the French army. M. Jollion notes with a delightful freshness of interest the primitive Egyptian methods of agriculture; the waterwheels of diverse kinds turned with a constant groaning by ox or mule, the absence of windmills, the heavy wooden ploughs, the flooding of the fields. The Kodak camera and the illustrated magazine have made these things the commonplaces of our pictures of the East; but yet after watching men for two years at strange exercises designed to increase their powers of destruction, it is a fresh joy to watch them at humanity's oldest and worthiest work labouring in the old way.

Our guide, feeling, no doubt, that the question is expected of him, asks when the war will be ended. He tells us that the people are wretched and food is dear. The complaint, we know, is idle; for Egypt is the one part of the Empire which certainly has not suffered by the war. Never has money been so plentiful, and never have her products found so ready a market. Even Rosetta must be enjoying unusual prosperity, though no army is encamped about the town and few boats put out to sea. The hay, the rice, the corn, and the barley are carried up the Nile, where no submarine can get at them, to feed the army in Palestine; and the fellah goes on his way rejoicing and bearing his sheaves.

Outside the town is a famous mosque set on a hill, from which we look down, here on the fruitful plains of the Delta waving with green and golden crops, and there on the sand-dunes and the sea. Enthralled for a little by the peace of nature, we dream that we are looking over the Norfolk Broads and the fields of England. We would like to stay and continue the dream; but to-morrow we must return to the trenches at Gaza and the fight with the Philistines.

THE REDEMPTION

IV. SUMMER-TIME OUTSIDE GAZA

(JULY, 1917.)

I HAD been down the Palestine-Egypt line to Cairo in the hospital train, that lovely thing of white and red which by its luxury gives you almost a thrill after months of " bivvies " and dug-outs. You travel in a car of cots and easy chairs with such comfort as the *wagon-lit* has not yet devised; you have luncheon with all sorts of half-forgotten delicacies; the smiling steward offers you drinks at every hour; a generous Red Cross Society presents you with a dainty wallet containing just the things you want—sweets, handkerchiefs, toothbrush, paper and pencil,—and the train runs so smoothly that you hardly know you are crossing Sinai once more.

After six weeks I came up the line again from Kantara to the railhead on the night " sleeping-car " passenger train, which is timed to do the journey in twelve hours, and keeps its time. The sleeping-car consists of hanging shelves, with a few leather cushions, in which some 30 officers doss for the night; and as there are no restaurants, so far, at the stations of the Trans-Continental line, we all come prepared to picnic, and the floor of the carriage in the morning is like the Blackpool beach after a Bank Holiday. The tugging and creaking of the couplings wake you at each station and forcefully recall each stage of the year's trek, and the year's wanderings in the wilderness, before we reach our destination. But the difference between the journey out and the journey back is not as striking as the difference between the scene which I left and the scene to which I returned.

When I went down the line the plain beyond the railhead, stretching away to the Gaza river and beyond, was populous with camps and tents and horse-lines and waggons that dotted the barley fields, a blue lagoon was set between the palm trees and the sand-dunes, and the ground sparkled and was fragrant with wild flowers. But oh! the heavy change now. Spring has gone! The barley has all been cut, and the ground is brown and burnt; the lagoon has almost dried up, or perhaps it has been drunk up by the myriad horses and camels; and the camps and tents have altogether disappeared from view. It is partly because our troops have gone forward since the second attack on Gaza and are now nearer the Turkish defences, but principally it is that they have gone underground.

The Egyptian Expeditionary Force at last has had to follow the example of the other British armies, and dig in. After a year and a half on the desert sands pursuing an elusive foe it has met him face to face; and straightway both sides have been forced to hide. We have descended, in fact, to trench warfare. The British and the Turks confront each other—below the ground—on a line of some fifteen miles from the sea along ridges half encircling Gaza, and thence south-eastwards to Hareni and the hills which overlook Beersheba. They are waging the thorough trench warfare, with all its regular incidents, the early morning and the evening artillery "strafes," the saps and the tunnellings, and the night raids. But so far we have escaped the hideousness of the model on the western front. There is no heartless desolation around, no diabolical overturning of the face of the land. Behind both lines are green orchards, and even the little farmhouses are allowed to stand, though they are respectfully recognised as "unhealthy" spots. No Man's Land is still green, and as the line is long but not deep the ugly business of the fighting machine is decently localised. When the men in the front trenches are changed and come into billets they merely march back a few miles and camp in one of the wadis which scar the country and are tolerably shell-proof and bomb-proof. A few fortunate ones are sent to rest camps on the seashore.

There is, indeed, something artificial in the firing which does go on. It is managed with a deliberation and a carefulness that is strange to the deafening fury of war as we read of it elsewhere. The guns seem to say, "We must have a little practice, so here goes; but please get out of the way till we are finished." Occasionally when there is a raid or an attack, and we are about to rush a trench, there is, of course, a bigger rattle. The heavy guns boom continuously, the light guns clatter, and the rifles ping, and if it is a night show there is a fine display of fireworks. But these things are rare, and for the most part we lead a peaceful life, somewhat cramped and somewhat bored, while we wait for our chance to drive out the Turk.

We are better off on the whole than we were during the summer of last year, though we are further off from the leave-cities and have the Blighty mail but once a fortnight. Then we were in the desert scorched and parched, constantly digging, but only so as to have to dig again in the same place or somewhere further on. Now we are in a country which is still green—in parts,—and have the beauty of trees and grass-covered hills. We are fanned every day by the breezes of the sea, we have a definite line to hold, we have an enemy that we can see occasionally.

We dwell in the land once sacred to Baalzebub, the Lord of the Flies; but perhaps because of the virtue of the Sanitary Section, or perhaps because of the strips of white muslin and fly netting which a generous commissariat issues to us, the flies seem to have lost their terrors.

And if the Turks choose to celebrate Ramadan this year, as they did last year, by an attack on our position, we shall not be sorry; and we are confident that we shall knock them at least as badly as we knocked them at Romani. If they do not come to the attack we trust that we shall go forth and get a little farther into the Promised Land. On a fine day in the latter part of the afternoon, when the earth is lovely and the sky clear, those who are posted on the hills to the east of Gaza can sometimes see gleaming in the far distance a white tower. It is the belfry of the Russian buildings on the Mount of Olives just outside Jerusalem, and for us it is the magnet that draws us on to redeem the Holy City.

THE REDEMPTION

V. THE RIVER OF GAZA

(SEPTEMBER, 1917)

THE river of Gaza, or the Wadi Guzzeh, as it is called on the maps, is to the Palestine front what the River Somme was for so long to the western front. A few miles ahead of its serpentine meanderings, from the sea to the mountainous backbone of the Holy Land, run the lines of trenches which cover the armies attacking and defending Gaza, now in deed as well as in name " a Strong Place."

It is not indeed a full, broad stream like the river of the western front, but for the most part a dry river-bed hollowed between steep banks. In the summer a thin silvery streak of water runs between the stones, and here and there widens to a pool fringed with reeds and oleanders. In the winter, when the rains pour down from the hills, it is said to be a rushing torrent which overflows its banks and tears through the sandy soil to the sea.

The Wadi Guzzeh is a narrow ditch in comparison with the Wadi El-Arish, which sprawls out at its mouth a fair half-mile in breadth.

But for that reason it is more headlong. At Shellal, where the Turkish army had taken up its main position to meet our advance in March, it falls in regular rapids. The name Shellal, in fact, is the Arabic for a fall; and here, as at the more famous Shellal above Assouan, British engineers will one day construct a dam to bring a new fertility to the country around.

The river of Gaza runs in curious and devious windings from its source above the Byzantine ruins of Khalassa to the sea, and all the way it is full of history. It has been at all periods the defensive line between Syria and Egypt, along which the armies of the Pharaohs faced the hordes of the Hittites, Assyrians met Egyptians, Selucid conquerors countered the Ptolemies, and Crusaders fought with Saracens; and now, for nearly six months, Britons and Turks have fought each other here. The relics of war are imprinted on its banks. Tracing its career backwards, at its mouth we find large deep caves now inhabited by owls, but once the "dug-outs" of warriors. Then passing Om Djerrar, the Gerar of the Bible, where Abraham and Isaac dwelt, we come to the fastness of Tel-el-Djemmi. It is a towering earthwork where man's hand has improved on nature. Our amateur antiquaries declare it to be a Crusader's bastion, because the skeleton of a man was found there with crossed knees. At Shellal, a few miles beyond, our amateur archæologists, to wit a squadron of Anzac cavalry, lighted on a splendid mosaic pavement, with a design and an inscription which proclaimed it Byzantine of the early centuries of the Christian era. The pavement was lying half exposed in one of the Turkish prepared positions, and is to find its way to one of the museums of the Dominions. Beyond Shellal, again, rises another of those dominating mounds, Tel-el-Fara, which is likewise ascribed to the Crusaders, and provides a providential place for an observation post. Thence the Wadi runs eastwards, almost at right angles to its original course, and is known now as the Wadi Shanag, and later as the Wadi Khalasra, after the ancient stronghold at the meeting of its sources.

The country on either side of the river-bed is a rolling grassy plain broken with sandy ridges. Beautiful in the spring, when the barley waved for miles, it has been sadly cut up by the engines, waggons, and guns which have passed over it, till it is now almost as arid as the desert, save where the shells of some enemy battery secure respect from our transport. Here and there a splash of bright green marks a garden or an orchard, and an occasional homestead stands out of the plain, while in the distance southwards is the wooded oasis of Khan Yunis, and northwards the enticing orchards and olive groves of our immediate goal—Gaza of the Philistines.

To-day the Wadi is the great watering-place of the British army. It is fortunate that the Turks abandoned their lines on the southern side, which they had elaborately prepared from Sheikh-Nuran to Shellal. Had they been able to hold them the summer might have gone more hardly for us; as it is, we are safe from the trials of thirst. Although its bed is apparently dry and stony, the Wadi has a wealth of water underground; and men, horses, and camels get their drink from it all along the line. For miles you pass from one enclosed area to another, each the jealously guarded watering-place of some unit, and hedged around with friendly wire and a *chevaux-de-frise* of waving tins. The inextricable maze of barbed coils we reserve for the Turks, but as a sign of property over man's most precious commodity we hang out these ornamental fences.

In front of the Wadi are our systems of trenches, skilfully devised along the slopes of the hills that rise up around Gaza and continually drawing closer to that objective. Batteries are hidden away in every unlikely spot and sequestered nook—irritable things which are ever ready to spit out fire when they see, or think they see, something or somebody moving ahead. It is at night that they vent their full spleen, and when they are all irritated together they make a terrible din. By the morning we usually find it has been much ado about nothing, and as a display of fireworks the illumination hardly compensates for the noise. But we have the consolation that the enemy appreciate it still less than ourselves.

Behind the Wadi is gathered the more peaceful apparatus of war—troops in reserve, ambulance and dressing stations, supply depots with stacks of forage and biscuits high as the earthworks that dominate the river itself, treeless parks of all kinds—parks of barbed wire in coils, parks of motor-cars, parks of waggons and limbers, parks of caterpillar-tractors. There also are the companies of camels in their thousands. Roads innumerable cross the river-bed from the peaceful to the warlike region, over which at night the motors, the tractors, the waggons, and the camels wend their way. The Seine at Paris has not more bridges than the Wadi has of these well-made crossings.

To-day the river of Gaza is a highway of the commerce of destruction, but in the good days to come, when the waters from its upper sources are properly husbanded, it will be a highway of the commerce that reclaims and creates prosperity.

GAZA (*April*, 1917)

The stony heaps of storied history
That dot the sand-cliffs by the Wadi's bank
Mark where the nobles of Palestine sank,
And dying Samson pulled down victory,
And venged his weakness and Delilah's craft.

Again by Gaza's stream the battle is arrayed,
Fire-breathing monsters leap from every glade
And breasting cairn and hedge with fatal shaft,
Like another Samson, crush the hostile line.

Oh ! Lord of Hosts, let peace and justice thrive
Where for two thousand years woe hath followed woe,
When England's flag shall fly o'er Palestine
And Jew and Arab shall together strive
To make their land with milk and honey flow

THE REDEMPTION

VI. A PALESTINE PLAYGROUND

(OCTOBER, 1917)

THE British army outside Gaza has its holiday at the seaside. All along the beach from the old Turco-Egyptian frontier at Rafa to our trenches facing Gaza, a distance of some fifteen miles, runs a line of camps and a vista of tents. And here in turn come the divisions for their spell when they are relieved at the front line. The south-western corner of Philistia is an admirable strip of coast for a war-time holiday. The sea rolls in to the wide sandy beach in regular breakers, like those that made the fame of Ostend and Blankenberg; but the *plages* of Palestine are more used to-day than the *plages* of Belgium.

A thick fringe of sandhills that seem infinite from the sea and stretch back in fact two miles screens off the noise as well as the sight of war. Nor does the enemy make any attempt to disturb the peace, and only our own buzzing aeroplanes survey the scene from above. Blackpool and Margate cannot boast such spacious or populous sands as those of

Khan Yunis or Tel-el-Marakeb. Some enterprising syndicate in days to come will doubtless establish here a fashionable watering-place and lay out the " Philistine golf links " over the dunes. The camps to-day are spread over mounds which cover ancient cities, and everywhere there are little clumps of palms which spring up miraculously from the sand. For water the men have only to dig anywhere a few feet, and straightway they have a well, or a sump, with scarce a tinge of brackishness. Napoleon, who passed this way a century ago, noted the extraordinary phenomenon that fresh water was to be had in abundance within a few yards of the sea when it could not be obtained 200 feet down amid the cultivated patches of melon gardens where the Bedouins used to have their settlements.

Animals as well as men have a complete rest—except, of course, the camels. In the balmy hours of the morning and the soft hours of the evening the long line of camels, each laden with burdens of some three hundredweight, threads its way over the sand Alps, where scarce any other animal will carry a load. The army in Palestine votes the Camel Transport Corps a blessing.

The Y.M.C.A. huts are far the biggest buildings in the landscape, and are always full. There is no pier, no casino on the beach, but there are military bands of the best playing the latest tunes. A famous band from New Zealand vies with another famous band of the Territorial division in popular favour. Bathing is, of course, the great sport. At early morning, noon, and evening parties of men and horses invade and occupy the front-line trenches of the sea and withstand the counter-attack of all the waves brought against them. Anzacs who have learnt to shoot the surf in the South Seas perform to the admiration of Scottish and Cockney Territorials. After bathing, football and cricket follow in popular favour. Tommy in the field knows nothing of a football " season." The whole year is sacred to the game, and not even the summer sun of Egypt and Syria can deter him. A big match between two regimental teams draws a crowd and excites cheering worthy of a League game at home. Cricket is a rather more exclusive game. Only the thorough enthusiast is prepared to fight the obstacles of pitch which the sand puts in the way. Boxing has a great vogue at night. There is an imposing Stadium wherein the ring is raised on sand-bags and floored by a great green tarpaulin, and here the Goliaths of New Zealand and Australia are pitted against the Davids of Caledonia and Canning Town. There are, too, numerous shooting galleries open free to the public, and the new amusement of bomb-throwing may be indulged in at the nation's expense.

In the life of play and amusement which

fills the day the deeper things are not entirely forgotten, for amid the palms which fringe what was once a blue lagoon but is now a bright green oasis of grass and reeds in the yellow expanse there have arisen during the last few months two churches, or rather a church and a chapel. They bring back the thought of home more than anything else in the country. One is of the Church of England, the other of the Roman Catholic Church. They are frail structures of matting and wood, without ornament or decoration, but in form and in appeal they are pieces of England. It is fitting that in the new crusade for the liberation of the Holy Land from neglect and misgovernment the only stationary buildings erected by our army should be dedicated to worship and prayer. It gives the touch of the Hebraic spirit which ennobles the war for a truer civilisation.

THE REDEMPTION

VII. FIRST DAYS IN BEERSHEBA

(November, 1917)

The first British troops entered Beersheba on the last day of October, and we followed them a day later. It was a striking procession which threaded the way along the two chief roads from the west and the south, leading to what had been the headquarters of the Turkish army of invasion of Egypt; infantry toiling along with their packs over the sand and the stony hills, and their following of baggage camels bringing their heavier burdens; long creaking lines of waggons drawn by mules that raised their plaintive cry as they struggled on; groaning caterpillars moving their tons of ammunition and food noisily but surely; rattling batteries forcing their way and asserting their privilege of the road over the toiling infantry and transport; motor-cars with staff officers pushing their way forward; and dense masses of horses and mules coming to the town of wells to water. As we approached from the south the town seemed to beat a series of retreats.

FIRST DAYS IN BEERSHEBA

We breasted a hill only to find a higher hill behind it, and crossed one line of abandoned trenches only to find another, till at last we stood on a brow which commanded the whole country and saw Beersheba lying, sullen and clouded with dust, below us.

It seemed extraordinary that the Turkish fortress should have fallen so easily. All the commanding hills, strong by nature, were stiffened with redoubts which looked as if they would have required months of approach. Yet the place had fallen in one day before a sudden attack of mounted troops on one side and infantry on the other. And the way was strewn with booty—ammunition of all kinds, and bivvies and officers' kits, which are curiously like ours, the same ground-sheets, the same folding tables and chairs.

Beersheba was unlike what we had imagined. We had thought to come to a white village set in an oasis, but in fact it looks like a small North-country factory town set in the midst of a bare sand-waste and limestone hills. The green pastures are to be seen stretching away to the east some miles distant, while the touch of romance lies further away in the misty blue mountains that form the wall of the Dead Sea. The dust of all ages from the time of the patriarch Abraham seemed to be blowing from the town. It was thick as a London fog and penetrating as a Scottish mist. We wished we could have exchanged our burden of respirators for dust helmets as we reeled in the whirl and eddies and were grimed all over, without hope of getting clean.

The town itself was half a Germanised settlement without the Germans, and half a Bedouin village without the Bedouins. It had been the headquarters of Djemal Pasha's army in 1914 and 1915, and the German advisers of the Turkish army had clearly set out to improve the place and improve the native mind with show of power. The Germans are fain to imitate the Roman emperors in this respect. Wherever they go they leave solid and imposing monuments of their passage. Only we it is who reap the benefit. Above the ramshackle, ruinous, and tortuous native quarters they have erected a suburb of strong and spacious buildings, with wide, straight streets, large plantations of eucalyptus and acacia trees, and an imposing railway station and depot. The dirt about the place suggested that this suburb had been given over recently to the Turkish forces, while the good condition of the buildings and the stores that were found in them proved that the Turkish residents had left in a hurry. The biggest building, indeed, which was apparently designed for a Government house, had been converted into a hospital in which thousands of Turkish wounded were being treated together with our own wounded men. The other main buildings were taken for the head-

FIRST DAYS IN BEERSHEBA

quarters of the different formations. In the midst arose the new mosque, a characteristic specimen of modern German art, half Orientalised. It was strangely like to the German church in Cairo, save that the minaret replaced the belfry; but Deutschland was clearly written all over it.

No civilian inhabitants were left, but a few Bedouins were wandering on the outskirts of the entering army undisturbed. The old bazaar was bolted, and the houses were all shut up, except such as were billets for our troops, and by all accounts the billets were not desirable, as the soldiers had to share them with many creeping things. The former inhabitants had left behind treacherous gifts: bottles that covered infernal machines, heaps of furniture that when you touched them exploded, live bombs and wires. The progress of the troops was marked by a running fire of explosions, most of which fortunately did little damage.

The essential thing in Beersheba now, as at all times during the ages, is the wells. The Well of the Covenant, Bir Sabe, from which the place has its name according to the Bible narrative, still gives its water, and there are beside it some half-dozen big Birs provided with modern pumping machinery. The Turks, when they made their hurried exit, had tried to wreck the machinery, and some of the wells were out of action for a few days, till our engineers, working day and night, had completed the repairs. But all the thousands of horses and mules and camels which thronged into Beersheba had their drink, though some had need put up with a long wait, and thousands of fantassas (camel tanks) were taken there daily and filled for the troops at the front. A picturesque contrast to our mass of khaki-clad troops around the troughs was offered by the few Bedouins in their sheepskins who came in from the wilderness of Judæa to their old watering-place with their camels and donkeys, looking and living as they and their ancestors have looked and lived for thousands of years.

The feeding of the thousands of men and animals camped in and around Beersheba proceeded as smoothly as if we were still in our summer camps. Daily the Territorial infantry and the Australian and British mounted troops pushed the Turks farther towards Hebron and Jerusalem over the pathless mountain slopes, and broke down their close lines of defence stretching westward to Gaza, on which they had spent half a year of work. But their rations were always brought up in time to sustain them for the next day's struggle. A great road, far wider than the *grandes routes* of France, sprang up from a little place of orchards and gardens, to which our railways had been hurried, to Beersheba; and along that road there moved unceasingly caterpillars and motor-lorries and miles and miles of camels, which in turn at Beersheba transferred their loads to waggons and other camels that went on to the front by devious ways under cover of the dark night. The boom of guns echoed around us from all the hills, becoming daily more distant. But we were undisturbed save by occasional visitations from Fritz, and he, too, after a few days, had enough to occupy him elsewhere.

Within a week Beersheba was almost a backwater, a mere depot for the advanced positions of our army. For we were on our march through Palestine, moving, maybe, to Dan and Damascus.

THE REDEMPTION

VII.I THE "COMPANIE" AT LUDD

(January, 1918)

Two miles north-east of Lydda, or Ludd, as we now Arabise the name, there lies a small Jewish colony. It climbs one of the lower spurs of the hills of Judæa, and amid the wilderness of mud villages which rise from the plain it is one of the oases that provide a welcome billeting place for our troops. To the Arab natives of the neighbourhood it is known as "Companie," the general title they give to all the modern Jewish foundations. They appear to regard "Companie" as a wizard who, with a touch of his wand, produces out of mud fruitful orchards and red-tiled houses. By the Jews the place is known as Ben Shemen, meaning literally the Son of Oil, the original settlement having consisted of a factory for making olive oil and soap. The present colony is the creation of the Jewish National Fund, which was founded by the Zionist organisation to secure land in Palestine for national purposes, as a kind of public domain. The training farm was established seven years ago, and

THE "COMPANIE" AT LUDD

the colony has sprung up around the farm. It is one of several institutions of the kind which have been preparing the way for the Jewish homeland, and training a people that for centuries have been debarred from the soil back to the life of their ancestors.

The large farm buildings stand out on the hill from the surrounding wood of olive and eucalyptus trees. The houses are grouped around the lower parts of the hill, and most of them are now serving as billets. But the training farm itself goes on with its work unperturbed by the presence of the troops. The Turks did some damage to the place, took their toll of the live-stock and the trees, and compelled a number of the young men to serve in the army. But the Russian Jews who are the workers on the farm are used to struggles with adversity, and renew a fresh hopefulness as soon as conditions improve. To-day some forty-five young men and women are happily and contentedly working on the farm. They live a communistic life together, like the craftsmen of the mediæval guilds or the undergraduates of Oxford and Cambridge. They form a society for work and pleasure, and take all their meals in the common hall, forming what they call a "co-operative." The young men are dressed in white smocks and trousers, and wear their hair long *à la Russe*. The young women, on the other hand, have their hair cut short, and though they have not affected the masculine attire of the women land-workers in England, their costume is sufficiently workmanlike. Hebrew is their language at work and play.

Despite the deportations of the Turks, the farm still boasts some prize live-stock, cows, oxen, and sheep, which are very different from the local kinds; and it has still some of the prize fowls and geese which are to improve the breed throughout the land. The fields, too, are quite a model of cultivation; and even in this fruitful corner of Judæa, where the olive groves stretch for miles, they form a purple patch of fertility. The war has indeed claimed one victim in this colony. A branch of the Bezalel School of Arts and Crafts, which, in Jerusalem, has at once provided employment for some hundreds of Jewish young men and women and given a new impulse to the artistic spirit of the people, was planted at Ben Shemen a few years since. Working thus in the midst of the hills of Judæa, where the beauties of nature and historic association mingle with each other, the craftsman could scarcely fail to imbibe inspiration from the outward conditions of his life. The stress of the conflict, however, has cut off both the market for the artistic work of the Bezalel and the sources of outside help, and though the main institution at Jerusalem has contrived to carry on its activity the infant offspring had to be abandoned for the time. But without a doubt it will spring to new and eager life now that England's protecting hand is stretched over the country.

The town of Lydda was in the early centuries a far-famed centre of Rabbinical learning, and its schools were visited by students from the whole of the Jewish Diaspora. To-day the Jewish schools in this neighbourhood are of another kind. They are training the manhood and womanhood of the new Judæa for life on the land, helping to make the learned student a capable peasant. When the war is over and Jewry sets itself to its tasks of reconstruction and resettlement these schools will need to be multiplied a hundredfold throughout the country; from them will go forth the new generation of Hebrew husbandmen and craftsmen to reclaim the land which waits for the people who love it and will give it their whole energy and devotion.

THE REDEMPTION

IX. THE REDEMPTION OF JUDÆA

(February, 1918)

The British forces drove the Turks out of Jerusalem on the first day of the Jewish feast of Chanuka, the anniversary of the entry of Judas Maccabæus into the city after the rout of the Hellenistic hordes. The coincidence is a happy one for the future of Palestine. As the Maccabæan victory marked definitely the defeat of a debased Hellenism which threatened human liberty and morality, the present British victory marks definitely the defeat of the debased German will to domination which threatened the independence and well-being of all small nationalities. Whatever the eventual political settlement of the country, the English entry means the opening of a new era for the Jewish people. It means also the liberation of Palestine from the misgovernment and subversive anarchy which for eighty years have wasted its resources.

The rapid advance of the British forces from Gaza has released the whole of Judæa in little more than a month. Within twenty

THE REDEMPTION OF JUDÆA

days of the taking of the stronghold of the Philistines the army swept over the Plain of Philistia, the smiling park of the Plain of Sharon, and reached the River El-Auja, ten miles north of Jaffa. Within another twenty days it broke the Turkish defence line in the hills from Hebron to the ancient Bethel, and left no organised band of the enemy throughout what was the ancient kingdom of Judah. The area restored comprises all the Jewish colonies of Southern Palestine—Castinieh, Ekron, Katra, Rechoboth, Rischon-le-Zion, Petach Tikvah, lying in the plain, and Hulda, Moza, and Artuf in the hills. It comprises also, besides Jerusalem with its 50,000 souls, Jaffa, which is the economic and cultural centre of the infant Jewish resettlement, and Hebron, which is a holy city and has a Jewish population of several thousands. It includes also the large villages of Ramleh and Lydda and Mejdel and the town of Bethlehem, which has a considerable Christian as well as Arab population. And the occupation means that the nucleus of the Jewish resettlement is saved, even if disaster should overtake the settlements of the north.

Within the country the English advance is taken almost as a matter of course. The Jewish people have been counting on it for a year, and they show no exuberant enthusiasm now that their expectation has been fulfilled. They are more excited about the formation of the Jewish regiment, of which tidings have reached them in a somewhat distorted form. They regard it as a striking manifestation of the national spirit which is their peculiar pride, and they enquire anxiously when it will arrive in the country to help drive the Turks from Galilee. Many imagined it was to come out under " General Jabotinsky," the " general " being a prominent Russo-Jewish journalist, who has had much to do with the promotion of the idea, but who holds in fact a far less exalted position in the unit. Probably many of the young men would be eager to join the ranks when the regiment arrives in the land ; until then the settlers agree that the redemption came just in time to save them and their colonies from ruin.

Menaced for three years by Turkish spite and jealousy, which occasionally broke into outrage, and by German arrogance and methodical destructiveness, which sacrificed everything for military needs, they were likely to have suffered the fate which befell the Jews of Jaffa when the British army had to fall back last April from the river of Gaza. But the swiftness of the advance paralysed the power of destruction as well as the power of defence. Save for Petach Tikvah, the largest of the colonies, which is situated on the course of the El-Auja, and fell into the no-man's land between the two armies for a period, the villages have escaped with a few shells and bombs and a few days of Turkish military occupation. To-day they are the favourite resting-places of the British troops, who find something of the joys of home among the gardens and villas and cottages. To the soldiers who, many of them, have wandered for more than forty weeks in the wilderness of Sinai before entering the Promised Land, Judæa makes a different appeal from that which it made to the parties of beef-fed tourists who cried out at the barrenness of the land. For them the Jewish enclosures seem on the whole, as they seemed to the Hebrew tribes who had wandered over the same wilderness, a land flowing with milk and honey. The orange groves, the vineyards, the plantations, which have somehow survived the drought of petrol and the wanton spoiling of the Turks, are a delight of fruitfulness, and the rich tilth is sharply contrasted with the stony, half-cultivated fells of the Arabs.

The colonies, on their side, have a warm welcome for the British soldier, who comes not only as their deliverer, but in some cases as their kin. For there are young men born and bred in Palestine who, having emigrated in hard times to the Antipodes, have now returned to their homeland in the ranks of the Australian Imperial forces. The Arabs, too, are quick to realise the difference between the new and the old army sojourning in their midst. They are reaping a harvest with their eggs and their half-ripe oranges—

most of the Arab population, adult and infant, is engaged in hawking oranges on the roads—and they are again ploughing with their wooden ploughshares, drawn by camel or ox, being convinced that they will have the benefit of this year's sowing, the first they will have enjoyed for three years.

The war, however, has already made some retribution for the harm and hardship it has caused to the country. Against the loss of markets and the destruction of much property and the felling of the scant timber, may be set the opening up of roads and railways and the linking up of Palestine with Syria and Egypt. Palestine is again fast coming into its natural heritage as one of the chief junctions between the Orient and the Occident. The danger is rather that it will lose its simplicity in isolation, which, in former ages, helped to preserve its position and influence. The Jews are already in the forefront of the work of expansion. During the Turkish army's occupation of the South a little settlement of them had found its way, or was transplanted forcibly, to Beersheba to work as artisans on the railway or on the water supply. The Jewish agriculturists, too, now find themselves placed near the main lines of railways, so that their produce will be carried to all parts of the land and to lands beyond. Jaffa is again becoming a port for the embarking of light ships, and some of the ancient harbours at the mouth of the wadis which have been derelict for nearly 2,000 years have suddenly sprung into fresh life.

The green plains to the south and east of Beersheba, which were thickly populated in the Byzantine epoch, have been given fresh opportunities by the Turkish railway to the Egyptian frontier. They can easily be put into working order, and are to be settled and reclaimed. But even before the end of the war something can be done in these directions to prepare for the new age and to make the redeemed land at once more useful to the redeemers. Simple measures of irrigation would immediately render large areas, now waste, capable of full cultivation, and a population to work the land scientifically could be found in the Jewish villages and towns. Moreover, there are still in Egypt some thousands of Palestinian refugees waiting to return to their homes. The Germans during their occupation of Jerusalem and Beersheba have done something in the way of town planning and building and tree planting, which shows what a little skilled direction may accomplish. The spiritual Renaissance which the romantic return of the world's most steadfast nationality to its home will bring may, in part, wait till the days of peace; the material basis of that revival may be laid in the days of war.

THE REDEMPTION

X. JAFFA REVIVED

(March, 1918)

In these days of bounteous spring Jaffa more than ever justifies her Hebrew name, which she has kept inviolate through the ages, meaning the "Beautiful Place." When the whole countryside is fair to look on, the town, with its red roofs and white domes set round its orchards and gardens, and its palms and cypresses on the hills that rise straight from the sea, is yet distinguished by its loveliness. I had come down the flowery slopes of the Judæan hills, past the shady avenues of Wilhelme—emptied now of its German inhabitants, but still preserving its German neatness—then over the meadows and cornfields past Yehudiyeh and Bnei Berak, villages celebrated in Rabbinical lore, and, lastly, through the orange groves. It was a progress of fertility and fruitfulness, and at the end the scent of orange-blossom and the more transparent blue of the sky which is the sea's gift, suggested an approach to the Elysian Fields.

The promise is not entirely realised, for

JAFFA REVIVED

Jaffa is still largely a collection of mean and dirty houses. Outwardly it is little changed. It has escaped the horrors of war, and during the last three years has even been embellished by the Turks. Djemal Pasha has desired to be remembered for good in one place, and an avenue bearing his name now runs from Ramleh Road to the High Street which is flanked by ornamental gardens and has in its centre a music-kiosk of the most approved and showy character. The avenue was the work of a Jewish engineer and contractor, and was apparently prompted by a desire to emulate the boulevards of the Jewish suburb, Tel Aviv.

Within the town the British authorities on their part have already introduced a measure of cleanliness and order, and they have cleared a road through the maze of lanes leading to the port. They have restored too, in part, the commercial activity of the place, and made it again a haven of big ships.

Jaffa is, however, changed from what it was a few weeks ago. Then its narrow streets were bristling with soldiers, and Tel Aviv was the headquarters of a Scottish division. The names of places dear to the Scot were painted up by the side of the names dear to the Hebrew settlers. Princes Street and Lowland Avenue were set against the Avenue of Achad-Haam and the Boulevard of Edmond ·de Rothschild. The Scots' pipes played to the delight of a Jewish gathering, while the professors of the musical conservatoire gave a concert of Russian music for their northern visitors. Now the Scottish division is gone, and Tel Aviv is almost entirely what it was before the war—the head-quarters of the Yishub, the Jewish Resettlement.

Just over a year ago the Turks, in a mood of panic and spite, drove out the civil population, and 10,000 Jews were rendered houseless. Those of them who had the good fortune to take refuge in the South of Palestine have been able since the English occupation to return to their homes, and three or four thousand are now back. Their houses had been little damaged, and the spirit which made the place has been quickened by the fresh hope of the congregation of Israel. True, the chief pride of the Jewish townlet, the Gymnasium or High School, is still used as a military hospital, and one school has now to suffice for a community which used to boast half a dozen. And in the main street, where formerly a half-score of dentists had their tables, there are now as many barbers' signs, a survival of the conditions in which the dentist's art is provided free by a generous army, while shaving is left to the individual.

Tel Aviv, though not yet restored to the whole of its eager life, has, however, a new distraction. The Zionist flag flies from the house where the Director of the Palestine office of the Zionist organisation used to dwell, and it marks the presence of a headquarters more nearly touching the people than any other. Here in constant session works the Zionist Commission which has recently arrived from England, authorised by the British Government to prepare the way for the national resettlement. The Commission is the earnest of the Jewish repatriation. Its arrival at this stage means that through England's noble impulse the Jews are recognised by the Allies as the people who have a paramount interest in the living Palestine, and the capacity to restore the land to its fitting place in civilisation. The erection of Tel Aviv is one of the evidences of that capacity. And as a young Jewess who lives there said: " Not only is the place good, but the life in it is very good." It is one of the principal tasks of the Commission to spread the spirit of the founders of Tel Aviv over the whole of the country that has been redeemed from the Turks.

As I stood on the balcony of the house overlooking the townlet, which when I saw Jaffa first, ten years ago, had been nothing but sand-dunes, I remembered the last time I was there, a few months before the outbreak of the war. Doctor Ruppin, the director of the Palestine Bureau, had brought out a telescope, and we looked through it at the moon and the stars. He was used to seeking peace and rest in this way from all the worrying cares of the world. The moon was in her first quarter, and, gazing through the telescope, I saw beyond the thin golden crescent the rest of the orb, touched with the light and relieved from the surrounding blackness. The sight blended strikingly with my thoughts concerning Palestine. During the last twenty years the Jews had opened a new era in the history of Palestine. As yet only a small portion of the country was lighted up by Jewish effort, but the rest, though still in semi-darkness, exhibited to the gaze of the faithful a reflection of the light which shone from the smaller part, and gave a suggestion of beauty of the whole which would be manifest when the Revival was fully achieved.

Despite the gathering of terrible storms the light has never been eclipsed. It has continued so to extend its illumination that if the Jewish people will rise to-day to the height of their opportunity they may hope to see the perfection of the full orb.

THE REDEMPTION

XI. JERUSALEM REVISITED

(MARCH, 1918)

JERUSALEM is still, as the Psalmist describes it, builded as a city that is compact together. Though it spreads untidily outside the Crusaders' walls, it is a small place, and can be taken in at a glance from the Mount of Olives or Mount Zion. Outwardly the city has changed little during the years of war. There has been a little widening of parts of the Jaffa road, and there are trenches and gun emplacements on the Mount of Olives and Mount Scopus, where invading armies in former ages have often been encamped. But there is a striking change in the character of the place and in the people that throng its narrow ways.

The city within the walls is still a religious preserve, screened off from the common world, and into which the soldier can only enter if he has a special pass. But without the walls the soldiers have taken possession of nearly all the places where the various religious bodies had their abode. The supply depôt flounders in the mud of the courtyard of a Jewish school; the headquarters of a division are lodged in the house of an English missionary society; the Russian religious buildings, which dominate the suburbs around the Jaffa road, are now turned into a big military hospital; the Abyssinian Palace is the home of English nursing sisters; and the French convent, where the Turkish army had its offices, is still given over to the services of war, and has a French guard posted over it. Officers and men are billeted in houses and schools, and the horses and mules find shelter in the gardens. Along the Jaffa road tea-shops invite our soldiers with signboards in strange English to partake of tea, cakes, and sweets. Just outside the Jaffa Gate a primitive place of amusement has sprung up, where the entertainment is produced by the troupe of a division that boasts professional talent from the neighbourhood of Drury Lane in one of its battalions; and a kinematograph booth, which before the war had a precarious existence, has now a nightly crowd of patrons.

Gone are nearly all the monks and papas and nuns; gone, too, are the droves of pilgrims and the Baedeker-led tourists and the shouting donkey-boys. Cook's offices, which were the hub of the visitors' wanderings, are closed; but the shop of the American colony has been opened again, and does a flourishing business in Palestine souvenirs and photographs. The Turkish Crescent and Star have not yet been painted out from the Jaffa Gate, and it is a remarkable sign of the liberality of our occupation that the Arab police, clad in their dark blue serge and Astrakhan caps, keep order for us, as they did for the Turks. One curious reminder of home stares at the Englishman as he enters the city—the clock surmounting the tawdry tower within the gate, which bears on its face the legend " Dent, Cockspur Street, London."

Within the walled city business seems to be going on as vigorously as before, and with no less chaffering. In the bazaars that thread the dark arcades the Arab and Jewish pedlars have still their little stalls; the clothes market round the Church of the Sepulchre draws its wonted crowd of sellers and buyers; and in one the street of modern shops the merchants bring out anew their wares of olive-wood and mother-of-pearl for the customers whom a kindly Providence has sent them after their lean years. We proceed to the Haram, the holy area, in the midst of which rises the Mosque of Omar. French Mohammedan soldiers guard its portals in place of the former Turkish soldiers, and the soothing greens and the quiet paths are now open to persons of all creeds. The Mosques of Omar and El-Aksa which are set on the pleasant gardens are, however, reserved more strictly than ever for the Mohammedan. Not even the consular kavass can conduct the non-Moslem sightseers over the beauties of the sanctuary; but the Egyptian camel-driver or labourer who has accompanied our armies may now make his pilgrimage between his hours of work and become a "Hadgi" when he returns to his village. The Church of the Sepulchre, likewise guarded by Moslems in respect for the ancient tradition, is also closed to the soldier.

We leave the town by the Gate of St. Stephen and cross the Vale of Gehenna to the Mount of Olives to get the view over the city and Judæa—one of the most impressive views in the whole world. The monks are gone from the Russian monastery that stands on the Mount; but you may still climb the crazy spiral staircase of the Russian tower, and survey half Palestine. Of the war there is little trace as you gaze. One of our big guns occasionally booms over the wilderness, searching for some Turkish position; and through glasses you can see Turkish lorries and waggons moving round Jericho, and you can see little dots on the Dead Sea which are motor-boats. But the British and Turkish lines, which run by the Jericho road, are hidden away in the clefts of the rock.

On one of the spurs of the Mount of Olives there rises a palatial building, which served as the headquarters of the Turkish army till we disturbed them. It is the Kaiserin Augusta Victoria Hospital, one of the five religious bastions which the Germans erected around the town " in majorem Die gloriam." From without it looks like some Rhine castle and cathedral combined. Within the decorations and the appointments are rich to the point of luxury. The height of splendour is reached in the chapel, which is a blaze of mosaics and coloured marbles. One of the largest mosaics shows the Kaiser and his spouse presenting the hospital to God, seated on their throne. The Kaiser is clad in the garb of a Roman Emperor, but is unmistakably Wilhelm II, for the name is written underneath to prevent error. Pruned of the ostentation, the hospital would make a worthy setting for that hall of peace and international justice which, when the war is over, might surely be established in Jerusalem. The city which is the religious capital of half the world is the fitting place where men should judge the causes of the nations with righteousness.

The population has fallen to less than half of what it was before the war, when it comprised 60,000 Jews and 40,000 others. That is the most eloquent testimony to the sufferings of the last three years. A tithe may have left the country or been deported; the rest have died of disease or starvation. Always dependent for its food and the money to buy it on countries abroad, the people of Jerusalem were cut off at once from nearly the whole of Europe and from America, and a prey to

T

Turkish military exactions. In spite of all this, it is a notable fact that the Jewish communities did not allow their schools to suffer. The kindergartens, the boys' and girls' schools, the teachers' college, the whole edifice of Hebrew education which was raised with such high hopes a few years before the war, has survived the storm and stress, and is still upright. In many cases the school buildings have been changed, perforce; in several the children are now sharing the premises with the troops. But the cramped spaces cannot impair their enthusiasm, which has been stirred anew by Mr. Balfour's declaration that England will do what she can to make Palestine a Jewish homeland. *Hatekvah*, "The Hope," is the name of the Jewish Nationalists' anthem, and hopefulness springs eternal in the Jewish breast. The more adverse the conditions, the deeper the faith in the approach of the better age.

THE REDEMPTION

XII. A PALESTINE VILLAGE AT PLAY

(March, 1918)

We had been invited to an entertainment at the Jewish village of R——, which was being given in support of the Red Cross. Everybody in the neighbourhood was going, and as we rode over from our camp we passed the rumbling American carts that were carrying the gentry from the surrounding Jewish villages. We arrived half an hour after the time stated for the performance, but still half an hour too early. The Jews in their old-new home maintain Oriental standards of punctuality. We found a great gathering in the vast cellar of the wine-distillery, the biggest building of the colony, which, decorated with the British and Jewish flags and with flowers and foliage, made a fine public hall. The vintage has been scanty for the last three years, and no barrels encumbered the floor. Between one thousand and fifteen hundred people were assembled, one half of them officers and soldiers from the regiments in camp around, and the other half villagers, old and young, who had come with their families. The women and girls were in their best clothes, and very attractive they looked in their bright colours and their Oriental embroideries. It is wonderful how within the space of one generation the Jewish youth living on the land has gained an upstanding gait, clear, strong eyes, and a bright, fresh colour, which seem to be ages away from the bent backs, the sallow cheeks, and the hunted look of the Ghetto. All the Jewish part of the assembly talks Hebrew as a point of honour, and they are immensely delighted that Jewish soldiers from England (the land, as they regard it, of fullest liberty and decaying Judaism) should be able to utter a few sentences in their own language. The rejection of Yiddish, the Ghetto dialect, for Hebrew, the national tongue, is indeed symptomatic of the outlook of the new generation.

The entertainment began with a play, which was, of course, in Hebrew, and was acted by workmen of the colony. It was a Hebraic imitation of an Ibsen tragedy, exaggerated to the point of the grotesque. A Russo-Jewish student returns from the university to his home to be married, and learns that both his father and his uncle had committed suicide years ago. Convinced that his family is degenerate, he cannot bring himself to marry the girl he loves, and while the wedding arrangements are being discussed he leaves the room and hangs himself. It was not a merry story, and the audience was in merry mood, so it simply made no attempt to listen after the first few minutes, which was the easier because the inexperienced actors made little attempt to speak up. The one incident in the drama that aroused any enthusiasm or interest was the drinking of two glasses of stage wine by one of the characters. That at least was a piece of realism which everybody could understand; the rest was a mere homage to Hebrew.

The drama was followed by music, a violin and piano sonata. The absolute silence that reigned in the hall was a striking tribute to the power of good art, and the whole audience, civil and military, which had not ceased its talking and laughter during the play, was now quiet. Music is the art in which the infant Jewish Palestine community already excels, and it will surely make a great advance in the next generation. Then came a little speech-making by the chairman of the "Va-ad," or village Committee, who was one of the original settlers 35 years ago. He made an appeal for the Red Cross funds in Hebrew, and his words were translated into English sentence by sentence. Young ladies wearing a red shield of David on their arms made a collection and sold lottery tickets and sweets and cakes for the cause, just as the ladies would do in an English village entertainment.

Business over, we had more music, this time from the village band. The young men played wind instruments which had somehow been hidden away from the Turks, and the violinist conducted. The pieces were selections from the Yiddish operas—the Hebrew opera has yet to be born—which were altogether to the taste of the audience. The next part of the entertainment was a display of gymnastics by the school children. They looked admirable in their uniform, and they performed with the vivacity and eagerness which has made the Jews among the world's best entertainers. After that a comic duologue in Hebrew, translated from the Russian. And so till the early hours of the morning we went on with interchange of drama, music, and display, and ended with *tableaux vivants* of scenes from Bible history—David playing before King Saul, Solomon receiving the Queen of Sheba, and others. The scenes which recall the glory of the old Hebrew kingdom in the heyday of the monarchy are those on which the young Palestinians love to dwell.

When the entertainment of the programme was over at last the young people that were left—and there were still many—cleared part of the floor and started to dance. It is a good life and a merry in the village settlements of the Jewish pioneers. The young men and women know that they are remaking a homeland, and they rejoice with a light heart in the coming into their midst of the Power that stands for liberty and justice.

They are freed at last from the cramping persecution that some of them have known in Russia, and from the menace of Turkish spies, which for the last three years has been the skeleton at every feast. The words of the prophet of an earlier Restoration are being fulfilled anew: " The redeemed shall return and come with singing into Zion, and everlasting joy shall be theirs. They shall obtain gladness and joy, and sorrow and mourning shall flee away."

THE REDEMPTION

XIII. PASSOVER IN JERUSALEM, 1918

(April, 1918)

From generation to generation for nearly 2000 years the Jewish people have renewed the wish at each Passover feast: "Next year in Jerusalem." This year it was given to some three hundred Jewish officers and men on the Palestine front to fulfil that aspiration. The Commander-in-Chief ordered that forty-eight hours' leave to Jerusalem should be granted to men of the Jewish faith, wherever possible, for the celebration of the festival. The three hundred who assembled were but a tithe of the Jews on this front, to say nothing of the Judæan Battalion now training near Cairo, but it was a tithe representative of the dispersion of the Jews over the Empire and beyond. There were officers and men from Australia, New Zealand, and South Africa, and a couple of officers of the French detachment decorated with the Légion d'Honneur and the Croix de Guerre; two others who were Palestinians born, but were pursuing their studies abroad at the outbreak of war and joined the Allied armies; and English, Scotch, Welsh, and Irish Jews. It was like the pilgrimages of old, when the representatives of every Jewry in the Diaspora used to journey to the capital and take part in the Temple service; although, if Josephus is to be believed, in those days they numbered a million.

The three hundred were accommodated in the mansion—one of the large private houses in the city—of a Bokhara Jew, who is absent in America. All the populace delighted to do them honour, for the Jewish soldiers of the Allied armies were the symbol of liberation. They had brought not only relief from the Turkish misrule, but the promise of the new Jewish nationality re-established in its old homeland.

Last Passover had seen the expulsion of the population of Jaffa and the threat of expulsion from the whole of Judæa; this year was a very real feast of freedom and a turning-point in Jewish history. The welcome to the soldiers was organised by the Young Men and Women's Association of Maccabæans, whose aim it is to revive the physical prowess and well-being of the people. Distinguished by the blue and white sash, the national colours, inscribed with the shield of David, the national emblem, they were throughout the guides and hosts of the soldier-pilgrims. An official reception opened the feast, and was the occasion of much festal oratory. The heads of each section of the Jewish community spoke, all in Hebrew, for it is a point of national honour to talk the national language. The chaplain translated the addresses, and the welcome ended with the singing of the English National Anthem and the Hebrew national song "The Hope."

The Passover Eve ceremony took place in the large hall of the house, which was filled with the soldiers and a large number of their hosts. Each portion of the narrative of the Exodus from Egypt and each incident of the ceremonial had a fresh thrill in the historic surroundings. The words, which are typical of the spirit of the service, "It is not our ancestors alone whom God delivered from Egypt, but us and our children, who would otherwise be serfs," came as the expression of our inmost feeling as we thought over the events of this *annus mirabilis* for Jewry—the emancipation in Russia, the liberation of Palestine, England's declaration in favour of the Jewish homeland. And we ended with rival sing-songs in Hebrew and English.

On the second eve of the festival the Military Governor of Jerusalem attended the ceremony and aroused the enthusiasm of the men at the end of a short address by wishing them " shalom " (peace), the Hebrew greeting. The most rousing incident, however, of the feast was the march of the men through the old city to the Jews' Wall (generally known as the Wailing Wall), which is the Great Synagogue of Jerusalem. The march was followed by a great concourse, made up of the mediæval-looking Jews in their robes of plush and shovel-hats trimmed with fur, of vivacious Jewesses, eager to walk by the side of the soldiers, somewhat to the prejudice of good order and discipline. When, passing through the town by the Jaffa Gate, the men reached the narrow cobbled alleys of the old town, progress was almost impossible. At the Wall itself it took half an hour to clear a space into which the parade could be squeezed. It was partly pride which the local Jews felt in being able to show their neighbours that they had brethren who could fight, and partly the sense of brotherhood that binds Jews together everywhere, that moved the mass. And the soldiers in their turn were deeply moved when they stood before the place where the Temple of Israel's glory had been and recited the prayer for the restoration of that glory. They were privileged to enter the Haram, the holy area of the Temple, and to gaze on the beauty of the shrines which have taken the place of Solomon's Temple. From the Mosque of Omar they got an impression of what Jerusalem the Golden had been and may be yet again.

Jerusalem exercises a magnetism over almost all who come to it; even in its present lowly state it draws Jews together and makes them feel one people. The sense of home and brotherhood rises there irresistibly. Before we left the city we were each presented with a ring bearing the legend "If I forget thee, Jerusalem, may my right hand forget its cunning." But even without that reminder it would be impossible to forget this Passover in Jerusalem that opens a new era in the history of the world's oldest nationality.

Some sadness must be mixed with the most joyous of celebrations. The squalor and wretchedness of so much of the city, both within and without its walls, came as a shock to many of the men, who had imagined a place of palaces and splendid ruins, and found rows of hovels and rubbish-heaps beside the holy places, and hostels, and the hospices. But already the cleaning-up process has begun in this wonderful year, and with England's helping hand it will be speeded. Spring, too, was in the air, and men's work, like Nature's, can renew its beauty. So we parted, saying to each other, not the common "Next year in Jerusalem," but the other traditional greeting—"Next year in the Jerusalem which is to be rebuilt."

Laus Deo

INDEX

Aaronson, A., and scientific cultivation of land, 85
"Achuzah" schemes, 94
Agricultural Station, 85 f.
Al-Charisi, 15
Alexandria, Jews at, 6
  Palestinian exiles in, 172
Alexandrians, connection with Temple, 6
Alliance Israélite Universelle—
  found Jewish Agricultural School, 28
  schools in Safed, 143 f.
  schools, 156 f.
American plantations, 93
  colony in Jerusalem, 117
Anglo-Palestine Bank, 36
Arabs, cultivation, 81
  and Jews, 123 f.
  co-operation with, 206 f.
Argentine, colonies in, 30
Athlit, 82
  agricultural station at, 85 f.

Babylon, seat of learning, 10
  schools transferred to, 11
  Karaites driven from, 13
Banias, 148
Beersheba, British entry into, 248 ff.
Beirut, schools at, 150
Benjamin of Tudela in Holy Land, 14
Ben Shemen, 254 ff.
"Bezalel," school of Arts and Crafts, 169 f.
  branch at Ben Shemen of, 256
Bokhara, Jews of, 107

Cabbalists, in Jerusalem, 110
  chief seat of, in Palestine, 16
Cæsarea, historical associations of, 82 f.
Caligula, statue in Temple, 7
Carmel, historical associations of, 79 f.
Carthage, seat of learning at, 10
Chalukah, system of, 19 f.
  at Safed, 142 f.
Chateaubriand on Jerusalem, 105
Chederah, description of, 81 f.
Choveui Zion. (See Lovers of Zion.)
Christian Emperors, oppression of Jews under, 14

Christianity, rise of, 11
Christians in Jerusalem, 120 f.
  population in Palestine, 208
Church of Holy Sepulchre, 122
Cobbett, taunt of, 31
Colonial Trust, Jewish (" the Financial Instrument "), 35
Colonies, Agricultural, 49 ff.
  Jewish, in Canada, 54
  Palestinian, compared with non-Palestinian, 63
  government of, 68 f.
  smaller, in Judæa, 73 f.
  local patriotism in, 78
  Samarian group of, 79 f.
  in Galilee, 86 f.
  training in, 91
  working men's, 92
  in Northern Galilee, 95
  American, in Jerusalem, 117
Colonisation Association, Jewish, work in, in Palestine, 66
Committees. (See Va-ad.)
"Companie." (See Ben Shemen.)
Concordat and French Jews, 22
Conder, Colonel, estimate of Palestine population, 203
Congress. (See Zionist.)
Crimean War, effect on Zionism of, 25
Crusaders, capture of Palestine by, 14
  expulsion of, 15
Cyprus, Jewish community in, 8
Cyrene, Jewish community in, 8
Cyrus, return of Jews under, 4 f.

Damascus, community of Jews at, 14
  Blood Accusation at, 25
"Daniel Deronda" quoted, 27
Disraeli and Zionism, 27 f.
  "Tancred" quoted, 28
Djemal Pasha, war measures of, 185
Dome of the Rock, 114
Don Joseph of Naxos, permission to rebuild Tiberias, 17
  attempts at land colonisation in Galilee, 136
Donmeh, chief seat in Salonica, 19

El-Arish, colonising of, 37
  the Wadi of, 223
Eliot, George, quoted, 27

INDEX

England, Millenarian movement in, 19
  resettlement in, 19
  and Zionism, Declaration of British Government, 47
English advance, effect on Palestine, 191 ff., 258 ff.

Falashas in Jerusalem, 108
French Revolution, effect on Jews, 21

Gaius. (See Caligula.)
Galilee, schools in, 9
  new settlements in, 17
  colonies in, 86 f.
  training colonies in, 91
  colonies in Northern, 95
  beauty of, 129
  history of, 130 ff.
  Holy Cities of, 138 ff.
  north country of, 147 f.
  seaports of, 148 f.
  future of, 150 f.
Gaon. (See Wilna.)
Gaza, 223 ff.
  appearance of, 225
  history of, 225 f.
  future of, 227
  summer-time outside, 233 ff.
  river of. (See Wadi Guzzeh.)
  poem on, 243
Gilead, scheme for repopulation of, 29

Haifa Polytechnic, 162
Hebrew, struggle in schools for, 161 ff.
Herzl, influence on Zionism, 33 ff.
  and Basle Congress, 34
  opposed to small colonising enterprises, 36
Hess, Moses, on "Rome and Jerusalem," quoted, 26
Hilfsverein, schools of, 160 f.
Hillel the Second, 10
Hirsch, Baron de, and Argentine Republic, 30
  foundation in America, 55
Holy Sepulchre, church of, 122

Ica. (See Jewish Colonisation Association.)
Ibrahim Ali conquers Palestine, 23
Islam, rise of, 12 ff.
  Palestine under rule of, 15 f.
Israel, a nation, 3
  division of, 4
  dispersion of, 8
  under Roman yoke, 8
  love for Palestine of, 10. (See *Jews.*)

Jabotinsky, and the "Jewish Regiment," 260
Jaffa, growth of trade of, 32
  Hebrew Gymnasium at, 166 f.
  under British rule, 258 ff.
Jehuda Hallevi, 13
Jehuda Hanassi, and the Mishna, 9

Jerusalem—
  capture of, by Persians, 12
  revival of Jewish learning in, 15
  general characteristics of the city, 100 ff.
  the type of religion, 100
  situation outlook, 101 f.
  old and new, 104 f.
  Jewish population in, 105 f.
  settlement and colonies in, 107 f.
  Jewish quarter in, 108, 118 f.
  synagogues, 109
  sects in, 110
  Wailing Wall, 111 f.
  Christian, 120 f.
  influence of, 126 f.
  effect of war on, 189
  under British occupation, 269 ff.
  Passover in, 280 ff.
Jewish settlers in Palestine, 14 f.
  learning, revival of, 15
  culture, new supremacy in Palestine, 16
  resettlement in Palestine, a Christian ideal, 24
  nationality, revival of feeling for, 26
  foundation of Agricultural School by, 28
  agricultural settlements, 32
  immigration, stream of, 32 f.
  settlement in British East Africa, 37
  mission, 43 f.
  population in Jerusalem, 105 f.
  quarter in Jerusalem, 108
  in Jerusalem, 118 f.
  settlements, war and, 178 ff.
  people, future of, 193 ff.
Jewish Agricultural Station, 85 f.
Jewish Colonial Trust ("The Financial Instrument"), 35
Jewish Colonisation Association, work in Palestine of, 66
Jewish National Fund, incorporated, 35
  colonies promoted by, 88
Jewish Territorial Organisation, 38
Jews, oppressed by Christian emperors, 11
  persecution relaxed, 13
  expulsion from Spain, 16
  described by Lady Mary Wortley Montagu, 18
  resettlement in England, 19
  tendency to denationalise, 22
  contempt of, 26
  love of nature, 50 f.
  agricultural tendency, 53 f.
  and socialistic institutions, 89
  of Bokhara, 107
  and Arabs, 123 f.
Jordan, possibilities of, 199 f.
Joseph of Naxos. (See Don Joseph.)

INDEX

Josephus, on Jewish agricultural tendency, 52
  on beauty of Galilee, 130
Judæa, political history of, 5 ff.
  colonies in, 49 ff.
  redemption of, 258 ff.
  appeal to soldiers of, 261
Julian, the Apostate, 11

Kabbala, chief seat in Palestine, 16
  followers of, in Jerusalem, 110
Kalischer Hirsch, religious enthusiasm of, 29
Karaites, driven from Babylon, 13
  in Jerusalem, 110
Katra, life in, 73 f.

Lassalle and Zionism, 28
Lebanon, province of, 150
'*Lovers of Zion*,'' work of, 28
  Herzl and work of, 36
  opposition of, to Uganda Scheme, 38
  settlements in Palestine of, 66
Ludd. (See Lydda.)
Lydda, Jewish colony at, 254 ff.

Maccabæan struggle, 6 f.
Maccabæan Land Company, work of, 94
Maimonides, 15
Manasseh ben Israel and a resettlement in England, 19
Medjdel, a working man's colony, 92
Meiron, 144
Merchavya, Colony of, 87 f.
  experimental work in, 88
Mesopotamia, schemes for colonisation of, 39
Messiahs, false, 18
Mishna, compilation of, 9
Mohammed and Jerusalem, 12
Montagu, Lady Mary Wortley, describes the Jews, 18
Montefiore, Sir Moses, effort to establish Jewish Commonwealth, 23 f.
  Testimonial Trust, work of, 117
Morgenthau, Ambassador, visit to Palestine of, 46
  on condition of Jews in Palestine, 46 f.
Moser, Alderman, T. founds Jaffa Gymnasium, 167
Mosque of Omar. (See Dome of the Rock.)
Mount of Olives, view from, 115
Moza, foundation of, 55

Nachmanides, description of Palestine by, 16
Napoleon, publishes Manifesto to the Jews, 23
  connection with Rosetta of, 229, 231

National movement, rise of, 31 ff.
  University, plans of, 175 f.
  Fund, incorporation of Jewish, 35
Nehardea, sect of learning at, 10

Oliphant, Laurence, and Gilead scheme, 29
  on the Jewish pilgrim, 145

Palestine, historical significance of, 1 ff.
  importance to Jews, 2 ff.
  laid waste, 7 f.
  Israel's love for, 10
  invaded by Persians, 12
  sway of Crusaders in, 14
  condition of settlers in, 14 f.
  under rule of Islam, 15 f.
  description by Nachmanides of, 16
  conquered by Ibrahim Ali, 23
  Palestine Land Company, 24
  common goal of Jewish people, 30 f.
  Movement, opposition to, 38 ff.
  Jewish ideal and, 42 f.
  future of, 193 ff.
  natural prospects of, 195
  railways in, 195 f.
  agricultural prospects, 198 f.
  irrigation schemes, 198 f.
  industrial development, 200 f.
  Conder's estimate of, 203
  land of Promise, 204
  repeopling of, 204 f.
  Arab and Christian population in, 206 f.
  effect of the war on, 261 ff.
Palestinian schools, 9 ff.
  revival of schools, 165 ff.
  communities, decay of, 19
  village, at play, 275 ff.
Petach Tikvah, Colony of, 57 ff.
  Working men's settlements in, 59 f.
  Arab labourers and Yemenites in, 60
  population of, 62
  religious and social life in, 62 f.
  Sabbath observance in, 63 f.
Poalim (workers') settlements in Petach Tikvah, 59
  religious attitude of, 62
Poria, American plantation of, 93 f.

Rechoboth, Colony of, history of, 67
Rischon-le-Zion, Colony of, 67 ff.
Rome, Palestine under yoke of, 7 ff.
  seat of learning at, 10
  and Jerusalem, 26
Rosetta, the war and, 228 ff.
Rothschild, Baron Edmond de, visits Palestine, 46
  administration of, in colonies, 56
  and Rischon-le-Zion, 67
  Eveline de, School, 160

INDEX

Russia, effect on Zionism of persecutions in, 28 f.
source of new population in Palestine, 33

Sabbatai Zevi and the Donmeh, 18 f.
Safed, rise of, 17
  golden age of, 135 ff.
  and Tiberias, 137
  insanitary conditions, 139
  water supply, 140
  picturesqueness of, 141
  life in, 142
  Chaluka system at, 142 f.
  heights round, 146
Saladin, victory of, 15
Salonica, seat of Donmeh, 19
Samaria, Jewish colonies in, 78 ff.
Sanhedrin in Tiberias, 9
  of Paris, 21
Schools, Renaissance in, 152 ff.
  of the Ghetto, 153 ff.
  modern, 155 f.
  of the Alliance Israélite, 156 f.
  of the Hilfsverein, 160 f.
  struggle for Hebrew in, 161 f.
  religious teaching in, 168
  of music and art, 169 f.
  effect of war on, 172 f., 187 f.
Sedjera, Colony of, 91
Shomerim (watchers), work of, 71
Sidon and Tyre, 148 f.
Spain, Golden Era in, 13 f.
  expulsion of Jews from, 16
Stanley, Dean, quoted, 27
Suez Canal, advance from, 217 ff.
Synagogues in Jerusalem, 103 f.

Tantura, glass factory of, 83
Tel Aviv, British occupation of, 265 f.
Temple, rebuilding of, 5
  destruction by Titus, 7
  new shrine on site of, 13
Territorial Organisation, Jewish, 38
Tiberias, Sanhedrin settled at, 9
  revival of Jewish learning at, 15
  rebuilding of, 17
  colonies round Lake of, 93
  and Safed, 137
  description of, 137 f.
Titus, destruction of Temple by, 7
Torah, strengthening of bond of, 9

Transjordania, possibilities of, 97
Turkish régime in Palestine, 68 f.
Tyre and Sidon, 148 f.

Uganda project, 37 f.
University, plans of a national, 173 f.

Va-ad, in colonies and universal suffrage, 70 ff.
  justice administered by, 72
  assessment of taxes by, 72
Wadi Guzzeh, description of, 238 ff.
  the watering-place of British army, 241
Wailing Wall, Jews at, 111 f.
  Zangwill on, 113
War, effect on schools, 172 f.
  and the Jewish settlements, 178 ff.
  retribution for, in Palestine, 262
Watchers. (See Shomerim.)
Wilna, Gaon of, 19 f.
  and the Chalukah system, 20
Workers' Settlements. (See Poalim.)

Yarmuk, battle of, 12
Yellin, David, 163
Yemenites, immigration to Palestine, 33
  their way of life, 60
  in Jerusalem, 107 f.
Yishub (the return), ideal of, 20
  inspiration to whole of Jewry, 47
  sex equality in, 68

Zangwill (Israel), joins Herzl's following, 34
  forms I.T.O., 38
  on beggars and the wealthy, 41
  on the Wailing Wall, 113
Zichron Jacob, Colony of, descriptio of, 80 f.
Zion, Mule Corps, 183
Zionism, Herzl's influence on, 33 ff.
  opposition to, 40 ff.
  ideal of, 42
  tide flowing towards, 45 f.
  adoption by democracies of, 193 f.
Zionist Movement, use of, 21 ff.
  effect on Jewish life in Palestine, 35 ff.
  Congress of, 1905, 38
  Commission, work of, 267

PRINTED BY WILLIAM BRENDON AND SON, LTD. PLYMOUTH, ENGLAND

For Product Safety Concerns and Information please contact our EU representative GPSR@taylorandfrancis.com
Taylor & Francis Verlag GmbH, Kaufingerstraße 24, 80331 München, Germany

www.ingramcontent.com/pod-product-compliance
Lightning Source LLC
Chambersburg PA
CBHW070751020526

44115CB00032B/1642